GET A
LIFE !

# HOARDER
## to order

**Sue Kay**

**Hodder Arnold**
A MEMBER OF THE HODDER HEADLINE GROUP

Cover © Stock4B/Getting Images
Illustrations by Barking Dog Art

Orders: Please contact Bookpoint Ltd, 130 Milton Park, Abingdon, Oxon OX14 4SB.
Telephone: (44) 01235 827720, Fax: (44) 01235 400454. Lines are open from 9.00 to 17.00, Monday
to Saturday, with a 24-hour message answering service. You can also order through our website
www.hoddereducation.com

*British Library Cataloguing in Publication Data*
A catalogue record for this title is available from the British Library.

ISBN-10: 0 340 908033
ISBN-13: 9 780340 908037

First published          2006
Impression number   10 9 8 7 6 5 4 3 2 1
Year                        2008   2007   2006

Typeset by Pantek Arts Ltd, Maidstone, Kent.
Printed in Great Britain for Hodder Arnold, a division of Hodder Headline,
338 Euston Road, London, NW1 3BH, by Bath Press, Bath.

Hodder Headline's policy is to use papers that are natural, renewable and recyclable products and made
from wood grown in sustainable forests. The logging and manufacturing processes are expected to
conform to the environmental regulations of the country of origin.

Every effort has been made to trace copyright for material used in this book. The authors and
publishers would be happy to make arrangements with any holder of copyright whom it has not been
possible to trace successfully by the time of going to press.

The publisher has used its best endeavours to ensure that the URLs for external websites referred to in
this book are correct and active at the time of going to press. However, the publisher and the author
have no responsibility for the websites and can make no guarantee that a site will remain live or that
the content will remain relevant, decent or appropriate.

# CONTENTS

**DEDICATION** vi

**INTRODUCTION** vii

**CHAPTER 1 – Kickstart your decluttering** 1

**1.** Transform your self-image 2
**2.** Carrier-bag challenge 4
**3.** Ten-minute mini-challenge 6
**4.** 30-minute decluttering exercise 8
**5.** Commit to a new daily habit 10

**CHAPTER 2 – Transform your wardrobe** 13

**6.** Wardrobe clutter quiz 14
**7.** Clothes rail 16
**8.** Folding clothes 18
**9.** Accessories 20
**10.** Shoes 22
**11.** Bags 24
**12.** Jewellery 26
**13.** Sports clothing 28
**14.** Outdoor clothing 30
**15.** A wonderful wardrobe 32

**CHAPTER 3 – Blitz your bedroom** 35

**16.** Master bedroom 36
**17.** Bedroom floor 38
**18.** Tops and surfaces 40
**19.** Lotions and potions 42
**20.** Your bedroom oasis 44

**CHAPTER 4 – Clear your kitchen** 47

**21.** Kitchen clutter 48
**22.** Food 50
**23.** China and glasses 52
**24.** Pans and gadgets 54
**25.** Cutlery and junk drawers 56
**26.** Curtains to kitchen clutter 58
**27.** A fabulous kitchen forever 60

**CHAPTER 5 – Liberate your living space** 63

**28.** How ordered is your living room? 64
**29.** Knick-knacks and ornaments 66
**30.** DVDs and videos 68
**31.** Music 70
**32.** Paper pandemonium 72
**33.** Books 74
**34.** Dining area 76
**35.** A lovely living room 78

**CHAPTER 6 – Create space in your hall and bathroom** 81

**36.** Hallways and stairs 82
**37.** Bathroom 84
**38.** Your personal spa 86

**CHAPTER 7 – Spruce up your spare room** 89

**39.** Spare room 90
**40.** De-junk your spare room 92
**41.** Spare room storage 94

**CHAPTER 8 – Sort the scary areas 97**

**42.** Lofts and cellars                  98
**43.** Shed                                100
**44.** Garage                              102
**45.** Outdoor space                       104
**46.** Self-storage units                  106

**CHAPTER 9 – Encourage others in
          your household    109**

**47.** The challenge of living with others  110
**48.** Living with a partner               112
**49.** Kids and clutter                    114
**50.** Kids and consumerism                116
**51.** Pampered pets                       118
**52.** Household routines                  120

**CHAPTER 10 – Sort out sentimental
           belongings    123**

**53.** Are you a sentimental hoarder?      124
**54.** Memory box                          126
**55.** Presents                            128
**56.** Childhood possessions               130
**57.** Photographs                         132
**58.** Collections                         134
**59.** Inheritance and bereavement         136
**60.** Sentimental but selective           138

**CHAPTER 11 – Limit leisure
           equipment    141**

**61.** Arts and crafts                     142
**62.** Do-it-yourself                      144
**63.** Sports equipment                    146

**CHAPTER 12 – Purge your
           paperwork    149**

**64.** Paper clutter                       150
**65.** Stationery supplies                 152
**66.** Filing                              154
**67.** Financial records                   156
**68.** The post                            158

**69.** Non-essential papers                160
**70.** Working from home                   162
**71.** Good paper habits                   164

**Chapter 13 – Tame 21st century
           clutter    167**

**72.** New technology quizzes              168
**73.** Gadget overload                     170
**74.** Emails                              172

**Chapter 14 – Unload unwanted
           stuff    175**

**75.** Donating to charity                 176
**76.** Successful selling                  178
**77.** Recycling                           180
**78.** Rubbish                             182
**79.** Returning borrowed items            184
**80.** Re-gifting and swapping             186

**CHAPTER 15 – Select stylish
           storage    189**

**81.** Successful storage                  190
**82.** A place for everything              192
**83.** Storage mantras                     194
**84.** Storage products                    196

**CHAPTER 16 – Stem the tide of
           stuff    199**

**85.** New possessions                     200
**86.** Shopping habits                     202
**87.** Magpie tendencies                   204
**88.** New attitudes to acquiring stuff    206

**CHAPTER 17 – Nurture new
           habits    209**

**89.** One in, one out                     210
**90.** Do it now                           212
**91.** Use it or lose it                   214
**92.** The smile test                      216
**93.** Make decluttering fun               218

CONTENTS

**94.** Trust your gut                    220
**95.** Take time out                      222
**96.** Regular routines                   224

**CHAPTER 18 – Maintain**
            **motivation**      **227**

**97.** Support                           228
**98.** Simple living                     230
**99.** Progress not perfection           232
**100.** Celebrate your successes         234

**FURTHER INFORMATION**       **237**
**RECOMMENDED READING**       **242**

# DEDICATION

To Nick and everyone who has offered me such incredible support while writing this book. You know who you are!

# INTRODUCTION

Chambers *21st Century Dictionary* defines 'order' as 'a state in which everything is in its proper place' and 'the condition of being able to function properly'.

The powerful myth, 'Once a hoarder, always a hoarder', simply isn't true. No matter how muddled your home is today, you can change. There are many ex-hoarders out there who have wrested back control from a mountain of clutter.

We're immersed in constant consumerism, frantic schedules and a world that's rapidly evolving. It's hard to keep pace with the latest novel, MP3 player or this season's must-have boots. Ironically, while things appear to be getting more and more disposable, many people are battling against strong hoarding instincts and a lifetime's accumulation of possessions. Economic uncertainty, past emotional traumas and growing up in a family of hoarders all contribute to the desire to cling on to material goods.

But the ultimate question remains – is all this stuff making you happy? If your disorderly home is a continual source of frustration and embarrassment, the answer is clearly 'no'. *Hoarder to Order* will gently guide you through the decluttering maze and lead you to a more organised and fulfilling life!

# How to use this book

*Hoarder to Order* is a 100-day programme designed to fit into a busy life. The general rule is to allow approximately 30 minutes for each day's task. But everyone's hoarding habits are unique. If you have 200 pairs of shoes, rather than the average ten pairs, it's obviously going to take longer!

Aim to finish a task before moving on to the next one. But if you get completely stuck, put a marker in that page and return to it at the end of the 100-day programme. Remember, some of the goals in the book are longer term and can't be completed immediately.

Obviously some steps may not apply to you – if you don't have kids or a spare room, carry on to the next relevant day.

The key to success is to be pleased with all your achievements and to move steadily, day by day towards your goal of a fabulous home.

# Case studies

Throughout *Hoarder to Order* case studies and personal stories have been used to illustrate the highs and lows of decluttering. All of the stories used are true but personal details have been changed to protect confidentiality.

### How the book is laid out

**Chapters 1–8** are laid out on a room-by-room basis. Each chapter covers a specific room and is broken down into smaller daily tasks. Chapter 8 covers the scary areas that will need more time and attention, like sorting out the loft.

The initial focus is on dealing with your personal possessions. This enables you to gain momentum and confidence before involving the rest of the household.

**Chapters 9–13** cover family clutter and more taxing tasks like paperwork, sentimental belongings, and gadgets and gizmos.

**Chapters 14–15** discuss diverse and positive ways to dispose of unwanted goods and then create decent storage for the rest.

**Chapters 16–18** look at long-term habits that will allow you to remain clutter free and organised.

## About the author

I too have made the journey from hoarder to order. I used to be a real magpie and spent years blissfully haunting markets and jumble sales. I created the weirdest collections, from vintage Butlins badges to international snowstorms!

One day I suddenly understood how all this stuff was hemming me in. I wanted to simplify my life and rid myself of the clutter. I blitzed my possessions in a whirlwind week and was thrilled with the feeling of freedom.

I became fascinated by decluttering. I realised that hoarding, which is treated as a bit of joke, can profoundly derail people's lives. My degree in psychology gives me insight into the complexities people face in letting go.

In 2002 I set up my business, No More Clutter, in London and have loved the challenge of supporting others on their own decluttering journey. My first book, also called *No More Clutter*, explored the psychological reasons why we hoard as well as how to free up our lives.

I still enjoy browsing around markets and antique fairs – the difference is I no longer want to bring all the treasures home.

# The benefits of an orderly home

There are brilliant benefits to getting on top of clutter and chaos.

## Your mood will lift

Clutter is depressing – it's no fun living with junk and jumble every day. Your self-esteem and social life will improve when you feel proud of your home and happy to invite friends and family round.

## You'll save time

Time is a precious resource so why waste it looking for lost property? If getting dressed and finding your keys is a marathon every morning, imagine the fantastic feeling of being relaxed and ready to go.

## You'll save money

If you don't know what you own or can't lay your hands on it, you'll end up buying more of the same. Retail therapy may be a temporary respite from the domestic confusion, but will ultimately lead to over-loaded credit cards and a home full of surplus stuff.

## Less mess means less stress

It's stressful living in constant chaos. Restoring your home to a haven means that even on a down day, you'll be able to relax and unwind.

## Life will feel lighter

Discarding junk and outdated possessions will feel liberating and your home will reflect your current lifestyle. You'll be freed up to enjoy yourself, to explore new interests and to regain control of your life.

CHAPTER 1

# KICKSTART YOUR DECLUTTERING

I've watched many lifelong hoarders transform their lives, their homes and their habits.

The most important aspect of getting organised takes place in your head. Anyone who has lost weight or given up smoking knows that it takes time to see yourself as slim or a non-smoker. Thinking of yourself as an organised person rather than an incurable hoarder is an equal challenge.

## *Activity*

## The clutter tour

Take a clutter tour of your home, visiting each room in turn. Tune into your feelings about the debris in the hallway, unpaid bills on the kitchen counter, kids' toys everywhere and a bedroom that's more junkyard than sanctuary.

## Your self-image

♦ Consider how living in a perpetual muddle affects your self-image. Write down all the positive and negative phrases that come to mind. They might be:

'Clutterbug', 'like my father', 'creative', 'free spirit', 'too busy', 'too tired', 'slob', 'ashamed', 'overloaded', 'good memories', 'frustrated', 'I'll never change' ...

♦ How do these labels affect you? Do you feel that being a hoarder is a crucial part of who you are? Is it a way of rebelling against the images of perfect domesticity that we're fed by the media? Or have you felt too overwhelmed in the past and compared yourself unfavourably with your neater friends?

◆ Now choose new phrases to reflect where you'd like to be in 100 days. Maybe:

'Less stressed', 'more order', 'find my things easily', 'pay my bills on time', 'a wardrobe with only flattering clothes', 'streamline my kitchen', 'turn spare room into office', 'more room to be creative' ...

## Stay positive

Throughout the programme watch out for negative thoughts sabotaging your progress. You're questioning beliefs that you've held for many years and it will feel strange. It will also feel exhilarating to learn new skills and enjoy the lighter way of living.

Next time you say, 'I'll never get on top of this mess,' remind yourself that small daily steps are the path to becoming clutter free. You can do it!

## Your commitment

Psychological research has shown that signing a written commitment means you're more likely to succeed in making significant changes to your life.

I would like you to read and sign the following commitment:

**For the next 100 days I commit to setting aside 30 minutes every day to transform myself from a hoarder to an ordered person.**

**Signature**................................................................................

Make this your screensaver or pin it somewhere prominent to remind you of your goals.

'Unless commitment is made, there are only promises and hopes ... but no plans.' Peter Drucker, management pioneer and philosopher

KICKSTART YOUR DECLUTTERING

3

The aim of the carrier-bag challenge is to recognise clutter at a glance and to make snappy decisions about what to keep and what to let go. Clutter becomes so much a part of the domestic scenery that we don't notice a hideous brown vase any more or a box of videos stuffed under the bed. But every day we feel the draining effects of a disorganised, overfilled home.

## *Activity*
## Fill a bag for charity

- Start in the messiest room as this will be fertile territory. Quickly snatch and grab unwanted objects and put them in the carrier bag. Once you've looked around each room move on to the next until the bag is full.

- Trust yourself – if your first instinct is to get rid of something – it goes straight into the charity bag.

- Do this on your own when you have 15 minutes of uninterrupted time. Don't answer the phone or get sidetracked.

- Feel good about donating to charity. Choose a cause you support to boost your motivation throughout the challenge.

Once you have filled the carrier bag, write down how it felt. Were you frightened about making a mistake or relieved to have finally got your project underway? It's perfectly normal to feel wobbly in the early stages of decluttering.

🎯 **TOP TIP**

Use these criteria to identify clutter:
- unloved presents – think reindeer socks or crystal vases
- things you'll never use again like baby equipment or paperback romances
- anything associated with bad memories or unhappy times
- multiple copies of the same item – do you really need 40 mugs?
- stuff broken beyond repair is only fit for the bin – like a plug with one pin and all those lonely single earrings.

🎯 **TOP TIP**

- Don't empty out cupboards. This is a whole different project.
- Don't take anything out of the bag once it's in there.
- Never throw away other people's possessions. Your partner will be furious to discover a beloved collection of *Melody Makers* or vintage *Vogues* gone!
- Don't add valuable heirlooms to the bag. Their fate usually requires more thought.

## Finish the job

- OK, today's activity may only involve a carrier bag but see the task through by taking it to the charity shop right now. Otherwise you'll forget and by some weird clutter osmosis the stuff will get reabsorbed back into the household!
- For charity shops check out your local *Yellow Pages* or www.charityshops.org.uk.
- Reward yourself with a cappuccino or a glass of wine for doing a fantastic job!

KICKSTART YOUR DECLUTTERING

It's amazing how much you can accomplish in a short period of time. The 'little and often' method can be fitted into any lifestyle and isn't as daunting as attempting an entire room at once.

*Activity*

## Choose one of the ten minute mini-challenges

Set a timer and stop at the end of ten minutes.

- Clear your kitchen noticeboard of any takeaway menus, out-of-date notices and cab numbers you never use.

- Go through your cookbooks. If you never eat tofu or bake cakes you know which ones have to go!

- Get rich quick by hunting for loose coins. Did you know that the average home has £25 lying around?

- Search your underwear drawer and chuck away anything that's dingy or doesn't fit anymore. Don't forget holey socks or tights.

- Gather up the sweet wrappers, apple cores, coffee cups and fading newspapers littering your car.

## TOP TIP

- Don't leave any mess behind – put rubbish in the bin at the end of the session.
- If you feel overwhelmed, remember that decluttering will become more familiar and easier every day.
- It's crucial that you stay focused. Reading the recipe books is a distraction!
- Don't panic if you can't finish in ten minutes. You can return to it at a later date.

## Activity
## Review your progress

Do you feel pleased with what you've accomplished or, do you worry that it has hardly made an impression? If you're struggling to recognise your progress, use a Polaroid or digital camera and take a before and after picture. That way you'll see what incredible in-roads you're making into the chaos.

KICKSTART YOUR DECLUTTERING

Now you've completed a couple of short challenges, spend half an hour focusing on your linen cupboard. Decluttering involves lots of decisions – so don't be surprised if you get tired. Remember to deal with just one item at a time. If you feel swamped, stop for a minute and visualise the desired result – less stuff, more order.

## Hoarding habits

Hoarders are often perfectionists and hate to undertake a task unless they can finish it to the highest standard. But when there's a monumental amount of stuff, it's not always possible to leave everything at the end of each day in a perfect state. The key lessons are to set attainable targets and not to procrastinate. Keep up the momentum by acknowledging all your achievements, no matter how small.

### TOP TIP

♦   Buy vacuum packs for guest bedding. Store the quilt and bedlinen together so you can grab it quickly when a surprise visitor arrives.

## Wishlist

You may fancy upgrading some possessions like your pillowcases, or buying storage solutions for stashing the spare bedding. Create a wishlist in your notebook or your personal organiser. Look forward to treating yourself to some gorgeous sheets or fluffy towels.

*Activity*

## Throw out tatty towels and shabby sheets

- Work on a numbers policy – say two or three sets of sheets, pillowcases or duvet covers for each bed.

- Look closely at blankets, sleeping bags and eiderdowns. Give surplus ones to charity or, if they're too scruffy, take them to the textile-recycling bank.

- Examine duvets and pillows. Are they yellowing and stained? This isn't simply an aesthetic issue. Bedding harbours dust mites, which can worsen conditions such as asthma and eczema. Ten per cent of the weight of a two-year-old pillow is composed of dead mites and their droppings. So chuck ancient ones out and start again.

- Have your duvets had their annual trip to the dry cleaners? If not, take them today.

### TOP TIP

- Putting on uplifting music while you work helps to relax you and makes the process more enjoyable. Dance your way through the decluttering!

KICKSTART YOUR DECLUTTERING

Psychologists have found that it takes six weeks to fully establish a new habit. So it's vital to confront your disorganised tendencies straight away. Unfortunately there are no magic solutions – you'll have to do some jobs that you currently find boring or difficult. The good news is that, as the weeks go by, the new routines will become second nature. You'll reap the benefits of saving time and reducing stress. A bedroom cluttered with crumpled clothes or a work bag full of junk will be a distant memory.

## *Activity*

## The good habits quiz

Do the following quiz, answering 'always', 'sometimes' or 'never'.

- Do you put dirty laundry in the basket every night?

- Do you hang your clothes up at night?

- Do you clear your bag out daily?

Now choose one habit that you answered 'sometimes' or 'never' to. Your task is to commit to one good new habit for the next six weeks.

## The costs

Explore the cost of the way you currently do things. If you don't sort out your work bag you'll be lugging a heavy weight around, which could cause back strain. Not to mention the embarrassment of trying to find your train ticket with the inspector looming over you.

## The benefits

There are clear advantages to changing your ways. Imagine a lighter bag with everything to hand. That's your goal and your inspiration.

Add a reminder in your diary such as 'clear bag'. We'll be checking back in ten days to see how you've done.

## *Activity* Catch up

To make your task easier, catch up with the backlog today, for your chosen habit.

- Put all dirty linen in the laundry basket or, even better, straight in the washing machine. Collect up the dry cleaning too.

*or*

- Tidy away clean clothing that's draped on your exercise bike, the back of a chair or piled on the floor.

*or*

- Clear out your favourite bag. I bet you'll be amazed what you find lurking in there!

## TOP TIP

- ◆ If you find yourself struggling – because you're too busy or just want to put your feet up in the evening – remind yourself how irritating a lack of order is. Resistance makes even small jobs seem arduous. Stick a timer on and see if it actually takes more than a few minutes to complete the task.
- ◆ A common downfall is to miss a day and then feel that everything's lost. Don't get into a spin – no-one's perfect! Don't believe you're hopeless, a lost cause and that nothing will change. Simply return to the task the next day.

'Do something every day that you don't want to do; this is the golden rule for acquiring the habit of doing your duty without pain.'
Mark Twain, American author

KICKSTART YOUR DECLUTTERING

# Your notes

# CHAPTER 2

# TRANSFORM YOUR WARDROBE

TV makeover shows like *What Not To Wear* illustrate how liberating it is to ditch dowdy clothes. Decluttering your wardrobe will help you feel and look gorgeous.

## *Activity*

## Take stock of your cluttered wardrobe

Choose three items that you haven't worn in the last year. Spend a couple of minutes trying them on. Now do you remember why they fell from favour? Was it the droopy hem, shiny patches or sickly colour? If they're history add them to the charity or textile recycling bag. But, if you'd forgotten how stylish the stripy shirt looked, wear it now!

## Don't panic

Before you hide your head under the duvet, don't despair. Over the next nine days we'll be taking a step-by-step approach towards a fabulous wardrobe.

'I remember when pants were pants. You wore them for 20 years and then cut them down for pan scrubs. Or quilts.' Victoria Wood, comedian

TRANSFORM YOUR WARDROBE

*Activity*

## Wardrobe clutter quiz

Score one point for each 'yes'.

1  Does it take more than five minutes to choose an outfit in the morning?

2  Does your wardrobe contain:
   - garments that need dry-cleaning or mending
   - articles you haven't worn in the last year
   - clothes that don't fit
   - new purchases with the price tag on
   - clothes stashed in carrier bags that you're hiding from your partner
   - bargains bought in the sales or from a charity shop that you've never worn
   - clothes you don't wear any more but hold on to for emotional reasons
   - mismatched, tangled or wire hangers
   - miscellaneous junk that doesn't belong there?

3  Is the state of your wardrobe causing you stress?

4  Is it over six months since you last sorted your wardrobe?

**Your score**

1–2: Minimal clutter – this should be an easy task for you.

3–6: Things are getting out of hand – act now!

7–12: Your wardrobe needs urgent attention – there's no time to lose!

TRANSFORM YOUR WARDROBE

15

Aim to create the same ambience in your wardrobe that's achieved in upmarket dress shops. Imagine everything hanging beautifully and looking great!

## *Activity*

## Check out your wardrobe

Focus on your trousers, suits, shirts, dresses and skirts. Lay a clean sheet on the bed and remove everything from the rail (including hangers). Examine each article in turn and ask yourself:

- Have I worn it in the last year?

- Is it the right size for me?

- Does the tailoring and colour flatter me?

- Is it in good condition (not stained or shabby)?

- Do I feel good every time I wear it?

Unless it gets five 'yes' answers, why are you keeping it?

## Do

- ◆ Trust your first reaction. Listen for the unconscious sigh when you spot something you don't like anymore.
- ◆ If you're unsure, try it on and inspect yourself in a full-length mirror from all angles. Still undecided? Put it to one end of the rail with other 'maybes'. Pick one to wear every day over the next week. This will clarify if it's a keep or a chuck.

TRANSFORM YOUR WARDROBE

- Plan the best way to organise your pared-down wardrobe. Separate clothing into different categories – office, casual and evening.
- Use colour coding so that all white work shirts and black trousers are together.
- Consider installing a second rail to create double hanging for shirts.
- Only store current season outfits in your wardrobe. You don't want to be digging through shorts in mid January!

## Don't

- Don't leave jeans two sizes too small or oversized clothes in the wardrobe. Banish the depressing 'fat' ones to the charity bag. Store 'thin' clothes out of sight for six months. If they don't fit then, let them go.
- Expensive shopping mistakes hurt – but forgive yourself and recoup some money by selling on eBay or through a local second-hand shop.
- Don't ruin your precious clothes on wire hangers. Treat yourself to wooden ones for everyday clothes or padded ones for your flimsy items. Face all the hangers the same way to prevent tangling.
- Never overfill your wardrobe – otherwise everything's going to get creased.

'Never ever buy clothes you intend to slim into or – oh, the possibility of it – gain weight to fit into.' Karen Homer, style writer

TRANSFORM YOUR WARDROBE

An MFI survey revealed that there are over 250 million odd socks on the loose in the UK! If some of these are mingling in your bedroom with jumbled jumpers and tired T-shirts, get ready for some radical decluttering.

*Activity*

# Make over your muddled drawers

### Underwear

- Ditch the saggy stuff.

- Chuck odd socks. In future keep 10–12 pairs of socks plus a maximum of five pairs of sports socks.

- It's tough to part with lingerie that was a gift. But if you're never going to wear that red satin bra, it's simply clutter.

- Only give new underwear to charity shops – no-one wants to wear second-hand pants!

- Shocked by how much you still own? Stop buying lingerie or boxers for a while and save yourself a fortune.

### T-shirts

- Fading T-shirts get relegated to DIY, gym, bed or dusters. Be hard-hearted – only hold on to a few.

- Get rid of eyesores like black T-shirts that are greying or grubby white T-shirts.

- Divide your T-shirts into long sleeved, short sleeved and sleeveless vests. Then colour code them before folding flat.

- Cull your collection of T-shirts from concerts or holidays. Use your favourites for the gym and lose the rest.

**Knitwear**

- Chuck out shapeless jumpers.

- Opinion is divided about the best way to store knitwear – some experts think it's a crime to hang jumpers. Personally, I'm happy storing my less delicate cardigans on padded hangers.

- Wool jumpers can sometimes be resurrected by using a 'debobbling' gadget available from haberdashery departments.

- Allow yourself one beloved old jumper for days you need to curl up in something deeply comforting.

**Nightwear**

- If you're inundated at Christmas with novelty nighties or cartoon pyjamas, give them away today.

- One lightweight summer dressing gown and a cosy winter one is enough. The same applies to slippers. Do you really need more than one pair?

## Storage tips

- ◆ Use this opportunity to line your drawers with pretty lining paper. Add a lavender bag or cedarwood ball to keep moths at bay.
- ◆ A canvas hanging shelf unit in your wardrobe works well for folded clothes.
- ◆ Use underbed drawers with lids for out-of-season clothing.

### Folding made easy

Don't get frustrated if you find folding difficult. High-street clothing stores use a special folding device to get perfect results. Buy yourself one or use the cardboard inside a new shirt as a template.

TRANSFORM YOUR WARDROBE

**19**

Accessories can make an outfit look fabulous. They're a relatively cheap way to change your appearance every season. But they are definite fashion items and wearing dated ones can spoil your image.

## Activity

## Sort out your accessories

Untangle the muddled accessories tucked away in drawers to reveal the gorgeous ones you enjoy wearing.

### Ties

Hold on to stylish ties and disown the joke one with Elvis on. Take stained or crumpled ties to the dry cleaners. Some men prefer to roll their ties in a drawer while others like to use a tie hanger. Whichever you choose, make sure they're unknotted first.

### Belts

These should co-ordinate with your clothes and look good. Coil them in a drawer or use a specialist belt hanger.

### Silk scarves

Even the most sensational silk scarf can look messy. If they don't work for you, give them away! If they do suit you, keep only the most glamorous. Either place flat in the original boxes or fold them on a shelf. Hang up longer scarves.

TRANSFORM YOUR WARDROBE

### Sunglasses

How many forgotten pairs of sunglasses are lurking in your drawers? To stop this happening, store them near the front door so you can grab a pair on your way out.

### Spectacles

Every time you get your eyes tested have a clearout and only keep glasses with your current prescription. Otherwise you'll end up with lots of pairs dotted around your home, most of which will make life a blur! Opticians usually recycle old pairs plus spectacle cases.

### Hair accessories

These fall apart quickly. Chuck out any that are broken, tired or scruffy. Arrange the rest close to where you style your hair.

TRANSFORM YOUR WARDROBE

21

*Sex and the City*'s Carrie Bradshaw has many soul mates out there whose hearts lift at the sight of beautiful strappy sandals. Men's attitude to shoes has changed too in recent years. The days they just owned one pair of black and brown shoes are long gone. Today men treasure their collection of designer trainers and brogues.

Shoes are bulky so there's a critical moment when even the biggest walk-in wardrobe starts bursting at the seams. The aim is to let go of shoes that are uncomfortable or don't look good.

Even if parting with a single pair of shoes is torment, the following activity still applies to you. The more shoes you own, the more important it is to have them well-organised and cared for.

## TOP TIP

◆ Research has shown that the heart rate of dedicated shoppers soars when faced with an enticing new purchase. So walk away for ten minutes. When you feel calmer, owning your tenth pair of brown boots may not feel quite as thrilling.

## *Activity* Take a wild guess

● Guess how many pairs you currently own? Include trainers, boots and even flip flops.

● Assemble your entire collection, count up and see how accurate you were. Everyone consistently underestimates how many shoes they own.

- Keep all your shoes in good repair. Ditch the down-at-heel, unpolished look and get to know a good firm that can sole and heel shoes. Keep shoelaces, polish, protective sprays and brushes together.

- Work out an effective storage system. Either use the original shoe box or transparent boxes. Get a sturdy rack or a hanging canvas container with pockets to store everyday shoes. Men should ensure products are designed to accommodate larger shoes.

- Know where you stand on the comfort vs. beauty spectrum. Are you happy staggering around in four-inch heels that may look stunning but feel like agony? Then again, old trainers or 'comfy' shoes may not always be glamorous enough...

- Use a full-length mirror to check that your shoes match your outfit – including your socks and tights.

- Recycle shabby shoes. Many can be reconditioned and sent to developing countries or be re-used. In the USA they're turning trainers into sports tracks.

- Never buy shoes that are the wrong size just because they're in the sales. Much as you love your shoes, having plastic surgery to reduce your toes (it really does happen in New York) is going too far.

- Don't believe in miracles. Even the best cobbler in the world can't breathe life into shoes that are beyond repair.

- Use the one in, one out principle. Buying new black ankle boots means giving away a similar pair.

TRANSFORM YOUR WARDROBE

Do you constantly trip over laptop cases, briefcases and handbags? Are bulky suitcases or rucksacks cluttering up your hallway or spare room? It's time to stop bags taking over your home.

## CASE STUDY

Ollie liked to use a handbag for several weeks – then move on to the next. The thought of sorting them out sent her into a panic as many hadn't been cleared since her painful divorce.

I sent her off to make tea and tipped the contents out onto the coffee table. Once I chucked away chewing gum wrappers, caked up make-up, old tickets and torn flyers, Ollie was able to face the small pile remaining without too much trauma. She even found a 50-dollar bill and a lost pack of photos!

## *Activity* Keep the best bags

Gather up all your bags. Examine each one and ask yourself:

- Is it in good condition? If not, shoe repairers will fix a strap or a buckle.

- Do you still like it? Would you buy an identical bag if you lost this one?

- Does it function well? Bags that slip off your shoulder or suitcases with wonky wheels are incredibly irritating.

- Do you have enough storage space? Suitcases are often sold in sets so it's easy to acquire too many. Play the numbers game – decide how many you need and stick to it. Two large suitcases and one overnight bag may be enough.

- Put superfluous bags in the charity pile. More upmarket, designer or vintage bags can be sold.

## Clear contents

Sorting out the contents of bags is a kind of treasure hunt. I'm sure you'll find some gems as well as a lot of junk. A scout through a busy mum's handbag revealed 15 pens, two hair brushes, a bunch of seven keys (only two in use), six hair bands, two pairs of glasses, four hankies and much much more!

Empty thoroughly before donating to charity – you don't want a stranger getting hold of personal information like credit card slips.

## Upgrade storage

Find your favourites a good home. Do you need more hooks for them? Take care of your evening purses by storing them in a protective bag in your spare wardrobe.

Use your suitcases as extra storage. It'll be easy to remove beach clothes when you need instant access to a case. And don't forget to empty suitcases out as soon as you get back from holiday.

TRANSFORM YOUR WARDROBE

For many centuries it's been the cultural norm to pass jewellery down through the generations. Jewellery equalled wealth and a watch was a high-value item that would last a lifetime. The more expensive trappings of our bling-bling culture – the Rolexes, thick gold chains and designer rings – still have the aura of status and luxury.

Yet at the other end of the spectrum, every clothing store carries its own range of affordable jewellery. Just like chocolate, there's always something by the till to tempt you.

## CASE STUDY

Janine's apartment was full of watches, earrings, sunglasses and other knick-knacks. At the end of a long day she tuned in to shopping channels and rewarded herself. Her initial buzz was soon overridden by the guilt of spending money on trinkets that lay unopened in the box. Adding to the clutter, her in-laws regularly gave her flashy earrings that weren't her style. After agonising for a while, she sold the lot and bought herself a designer handbag, which she adores. She's also plucking up the courage to ask for vouchers this birthday!

# *Activity*
## Tidy your jumbled jewellery

- Sort everything into categories – watches, earrings, bracelets and rings.

- Dump all the useless tat like odd cuff-links.

- Inherited pieces can be painful to let go. Is there someone in your family you could pass unloved heirlooms on to?

- Stop squirreling things away for 'best'. Jewellery is meant to give pleasure, so wear a piece today that you usually save for special dates. Enjoy!

- Use original gift boxes for storing expensive or fragile items. Transparent boxes with separate sections work well for the rest.

- Visit the local jeweller to fix broken watch straps and replace flat batteries. Check if any of your silver and gold jewellery needs adjusting.

TRANSFORM YOUR WARDROBE

Whether you turn up at the yoga class in designer gear or hoard shape-less T-shirts for running, your sportswear will benefit from a sort out.

## CASE STUDY

Mark is in his mid-forties and has a demanding job. In his twenties he was very sporty and his spare wardrobe was crammed with cricket jumpers, rugby shirts and a motley selection of tracksuits and tired trainers. It was hard for him to admit he was getting older and couldn't devote endless hours to sport. Eventually he realised most of the sportswear was in poor shape and he let it go. The upside was that the process reminded him how much he missed cricket and he decided he'd go to nets in the winter.

## TOP TIP

◆ Don't start foraging in the garage today for your badminton racket or rowing machine. We'll be dealing with exercise equipment on Day 63.
◆ Avoid buying too much when you're planning to take up a new sports activity. See what you can hire or borrow instead – it'll save a lot of hassle (and money) if you decide surfing or golf isn't for you.

## Activity

# Organise your exercise outfits

The challenge today is to rationalise all your walking, cycling, swimming, golfing, yoga, tennis, squash, cricket, football, skiing and other exercise clothing. And don't forget the scruffy stuff earmarked for dog walking, gardening, DIY, housework or painting.

- Divide the clothing into separate activities like swimming or football. Decide how many changes of kit to keep. If you go to the gym three times a week, you only need three sets of clothes.

- Face facts – if it's five years since you last got on your mountain bike, are you going to do it again? If the answer is 'soon', be more specific. Make a commitment to take it up in the next month or part company with all the related gear.

- Apply the same principles to exercise clothing as you would any other garment. If you feel grotty in it or it's two sizes too big, it'll do nothing to increase your motivation.

- Separate exercise outfits from your everyday clothes – ideally in a different drawer.

- Pack away seasonal clothes – like tennis shorts.

- Donate your worn-out clothing to textile recycling banks. I like to imagine an old vest turning up in a new incarnation as furniture stuffing or roofing felt!

- Don't cling on to innumerable shabby clothes for the dirty chores like DIY or gardening. Keep just a few.

- Finally, don't forget to go through your sports bags and find what's lurking in there.

TRANSFORM YOUR WARDROBE

Hallways become choked with dust-covered coats that haven't been worn in years. An eighties' beige coat hangs alongside a faded linen jacket last worn in 1998. Coats and jackets are expensive purchases so we hold on to them to get our money's worth.

## Activity

## Overhaul your outdoor clothes

### Coats and jackets

- Raid the hall cupboard, the wardrobe, the coat rack and collect up your coats and jackets.

- Try on each one to see if it's still stylish and flattering.

- Say goodbye to once-loved items like a denim jacket that's more holes than fabric.

- Avoid the 'coming back into fashion' trap. Will you or your offspring really wear it in 20 years? It's doubtful – in the meantime it's taking up valuable storage space.

- Coats and jackets are bulky – only keep ones in the hall that you wear regularly. Check you have enough coat hooks for everyone in the household and a couple for guests.

- It's crucial to store everything away in pristine condition. There's nothing a moth loves more than a musty wool coat.

### Walking gear

- Make sure everything's comfortable and functional. A 'waterproof' walking jacket that leaks in the first downpour is useless.

- Pare down your kit. In his quest for the perfect walking boots, Mike had acquired several pairs he didn't wear anymore. He decided to pass them on to members of his local walking club.

## Hats

- Put on some music and have a fun session trying hats on.

- Baseball caps can look odd as you get older. Consider whether it's the right time to pass on your collection.

- If you only wear hats to weddings, hire them in future.

- If you feel ridiculous in hats, then one for the cold weather and a sunhat will do!

- If you reject some dressy hats, use the boxes to store scarves and gloves.

## Gloves

Ditch odd gloves without hesitation. Team one pair to go with each winter coat.

## Scarves

Delight in luxurious scarves that are a pleasure to wrap yourself in. Stick your college scarf or Dr Who one in the dressing-up or charity box.

## Umbrellas

Umbrellas tend to have a short life – either you leave them on the train or they disintegrate in a heavy downpour. Aim for a minimal approach – perhaps a black business one and another patterned one for going out. But if you've amassed dozens, have a few on hand and stash the surplus away for future replacements.

TRANSFORM YOUR WARDROBE

31

Congratulate yourself on all your hard work. Doesn't it feel amazing now your wardrobe is co-ordinated and everything looks sensational?

## *Activity*

## Successful strategies

For long-term control over clothes clutter, apply these winning tips:

- Declutter your wardrobe twice a year in April and October and pack away out-of-season clothing. Retake the wardrobe clutter quiz from Day 6 to see how you're doing.

- Don't let bad patterns creep back. The floor and the armchair aren't meant for jeans and T-shirts.

- Wear new purchases quickly. This prevents them being neglected in your wardrobe. Plus you'll recognise mistakes in time for a refund.

- Only buy clothes that fit beautifully. Some people buy smaller sizes to try to inspire them to lose weight. Unfortunately, looking at tight trousers often drives them to chocolate instead!

- Choose clothes you love. Don't settle for good enough, go for fabulous!

- Restrict retail therapy on bad days. We all need to coddle ourselves when life isn't going our way but limit it to a small treat.

- Accept that from time to time you'll miss the target and buy something weird. I bought an orange cardigan in a panic when I needed something colourful for TV. When I saw how pale I looked I had to kiss goodbye to the money and let it go. Sad but not worth feeling guilty about!

TRANSFORM YOUR WARDROBE

**Make your outfits work**

Buying a sharp shirt won't get you far if you've got nothing it goes with. Always plan an overall image. When you go shopping, take the shirt along to match up with trousers and skirts.

If time is tight in the mornings choose an outfit and make sure it is ironed and ready the night before.

'Always bear in mind that your own resolution to succeed is more important than any one thing.' Abraham Lincoln, US president 1861–5

## Daily habit update

Remember Day 5? You committed to a new daily habit – no dirty laundry on the floor, hanging clothes up or clearing out your bag. Congratulations if you've maintained it over the past ten days. It's likely to be less of a chore and a familiar part of your daily landscape now. Keep it up!

If you gave up or never got off the starting blocks, take a minute to consider where it went astray. Were you having an especially busy or stressful time? Or did you talk yourself out of it before you'd even started?

Don't beat yourself up. Instead recommit today and this time you will succeed!

TRANSFORM YOUR WARDROBE

# Your notes

CHAPTER 3

**BLITZ YOUR BEDROOM**

Now your wardrobe is out-of-this-world, turn your attention to the rest of your bedroom. We all need an oasis in our lives – a place we can retreat to and feel relaxed. That's almost impossible if your bedroom is knee-deep in clutter.

## *Activity* Bedroom clutter quiz

Kick your shoes off, lie on the bed and have a good look around the room. How does it feel? Are there mystery boxes on top of the wardrobe, a teetering tower of papers on the floor and a chest of drawers smothered in toiletries?

Not really the love nest or sanctuary of your dreams, is it? Check how bad it is by taking the bedroom clutter quiz. Score 1 for each statement you agree with:

1 There's so much stuff on the bedroom floor I can't even see the carpet.

2 The surfaces of the bedside table and the dressing table are covered in junk.

3 My exercise bike or armchair's sole use is for flinging clothes on.

4 It's seriously scary under the bed and I'm not sure what's ended up there.

5 I've more beauty or grooming products than the cosmetic counter at Selfridges.

6 Laundry winds up on the floor on a regular basis.

7 The clutter in my bedroom makes me bad tempered and I find it hard to sleep.

8  My bedroom activities include (score 1 for each)

- watching TV
- playing on the computer
- dealing with work projects
- sorting out financial matters
- talking or texting on the mobile.

**Your score**

If you scored over 7, it's more bombsite than beautiful bedroom! Start creating your oasis now ...

## Magic wand fantasy

Imagine a powerful decluttering wand that could instantly turn your bedroom into your fantasy room. What would you keep and what would you change? How would you create a personal place to unwind?

*Activity*

## De-junk your bedside table

- Get your project underway by tackling your bedside table. A mound of magazines, piles of books, vitamins, creams and odds and ends can congregate here. Clear everything off and give it a dust.

- Set a limit of two books and two magazines by your bed. Find another niche for unread or half-read ones.

- Dump all the junk that's accumulated. Only put back items that you actually use at bedtime.

BLITZ YOUR BEDROOM

Messy floors are depressing, attract dirt and are a health hazard at 2 am when you're trying to get to the loo. The minute you free up the floor, the whole flow of the room will improve.

## CASE STUDY

Carl lived in a tiny one-bedroom flat where space was at an absolute premium. As he pulled out papers and winter jumpers from under his bed a cloud of moths flew out. Everything had been munched and ruined. Unfortunately, moths thrive on paper just as much as wool. It was a blow for him but he chucked what couldn't be mended and went straight out and bought some storage containers and lavender bags. One benefit was he finally tossed out his college notes!

## *Activity* Clear the floor clutter

There are two ways to approach clearing the floor – you can descend to ground level and look the debris in the eye or you can spread a sheet on the bed and drag it all up. Choose whichever you're more comfortable with.

### The floor around the bed

- Floors are for walking on not for junk. Sort out suitable storage for homeless stuff that's taken root here.

- Never ever throw dirty laundry on the floor.

- Eliminate paperwork from the bedroom. If the last thing you see at night is your credit card bill it's going to be difficult to sleep!

- Do inspect your furniture – is there too much for the room and could it be better arranged?

**The alarming stuff hidden under your bed**

Karen Kingston, a Feng Shui expert, believes that junk under your bed saps your energy. Battered cardboard boxes lying neglected here for years are certainly depressing.

Either keep the underbed area completely clear or use it in a planned, effective way.

- Get down and dirty, and drag everything out.

- Open a window because there's going to be lots of dust.

- If you don't have built-in underbed drawers, buy lidded boxes on wheels. They're easy to manoeuvre and provide great storage for clean bedding.

- Take a dispassionate look at exercise equipment that's been abandoned for years – are you really going to use that abdominiser again?

- In future, resist the temptation to shove things under the bed. Out of sight isn't always out of mind.

'Bad habits are like a comfortable bed – easy to get into and hard to get out of.' Anonymous

BLITZ YOUR BEDROOM

If every surface of your bedroom furniture is shambolic, you'll feel like your bedroom is swamped. Aim to create gorgeous arrangements with your possessions and to display only beautiful and frequently used objects.

## Activity
## De-junk the surfaces of your bedroom furniture

- Deal with the top of your chest of drawers and then move on to each shelf or table in turn.

- Reduce the number of framed photos – the more you have, the less you tend to look at them.

- Reconsider the numerous scatter cushions you heap on the bed. I know it's fashionable, but not if they wind up thrown all over the floor.

- Curb collections in the bedroom – whether it's cuddly toys, books or sporting trophies.

- Be selective – while a few scented candles will enhance the atmosphere, dotting them everywhere will feel overpowering.

- Leave beauty products until tomorrow.

## Dust mites

Dust mites thrive in bedrooms because of the warmth, humidity and dead skin. A lot of dust is human skin, which the mites love to eat. Their droppings can then trigger asthma and other allergies. Sounds revolting, doesn't it! Excess cushions, teddy bears and fabrics make it tougher to control the problem. An unexpected benefit of a simpler decor could be an improvement in your health!

### ⊚ ◄ TOP TIP

◆ Get rid of unsightly cardboard boxes and battered suitcases littering the top of your wardrobe. Instead buy decorative boxes to provide extra storage here.

◆ Avoid covering every inch of the surfaces – clear space is much more calming.

Nowadays, with relentless pressure on both men and women to look attractive and youthful, it's not surprising that we're seduced by the latest anti-wrinkle cream. Even though our homes are already clogged with expensive lotions, we haunt beauty counters and scan glossy magazines, enthralled by exciting new products.

## Modern male trends

Men are catching women up in the grooming stakes. Lots of men have bathrooms and bedrooms stacked high with upmarket brands.

A recent survey found men were spending up to £190 on a first date with half of that going on clothes and grooming treatments!

 TOP TIP

- A recent survey found that few toiletries snaffled from hotel rooms ever get used. We all love a freebie but, before you automatically grab the body balm, ask yourself whether you'll use it or hoard it.
- Have you got various vitamins on your bedside table? How many of these do you actually take? Simplify your routine. Storing them in the kitchen near the kettle will trigger your memory in the morning.
- Don't open lots of pots of moisturiser at once. Limit yourself to a day and night cream.
- Once-used cleansers that don't suit your skin are clutter. These are unsuitable for charity shops but maybe a friend would like to experiment.

*Activity*

## Sort out beauty and grooming products

Decluttering may hurt a little as you realise how much money you've invested in cleansers and moisturisers that are now only fit for the bin. But persevere – it's short-term pain for long-term gain.

● Chuck anything that smells bad or has been open for years.

● Be rigorous about eye make-up like mascara, which should last a maximum of six months. Avoid an eye infection by replacing it regularly.

● Cleanse your make-up brushes and sponges today and then make it a weekly ritual.

● Declutter your lotions and make-up twice a year in spring/autumn at the same time as your wardrobe.

● Create space for your surplus stock. Store unopened aftershave or perfume bottles in a dark place.

● If you've got so many brand new products it's impossible to imagine ever getting through them, give some away as presents.

● Transparent bags are brilliant for storing make-up or travelling. You can see what you own and it encourages you to keep everything clean and orderly.

BLITZ YOUR BEDROOM

Your bedroom should be looking much better now. How close are you to your original aim of creating a relaxing, romantic space to be enjoyed by yourself or with your partner? What outstanding touches are needed to round off your bedroom blitz?

## Bedroom bans

These days many of us watch TV, work on our laptop and chat on the mobile in our bedrooms. All these activities bring associated paraphernalia like cables and TV guides. No wonder it's hard to relax surrounded by a sea of objects.

If you struggle to unwind at night, try restoring tranquillity to your bedroom. For a trial period of a month ban:

◆ computer games
◆ answering emails on your laptop
◆ kids' toys
◆ pets – perhaps it's time for your dog to sleep downstairs!
◆ your mobile phone
◆ TV and DVDs
◆ dealing with paperwork
◆ any work-related projects – particularly if you work from home
◆ the laundry basket – relocate this to the bathroom
◆ exercise equipment
◆ anything else that makes you wired and tense.

If that sounds too outrageous, at least try shutting one out for a week. Who knows – you might sleep a lot more soundly!

 TOP TIP

Keep a pad by the bed and if you find yourself worrying about tomorrow's meeting or the kids' schedules, make a note and then put it out of your mind until morning.

BLITZ YOUR BEDROOM

## *Activity*

### Checklist

Do you still need to do any of the following?

- Take curtains to the dry-cleaners.

- Dump ageing stained pillows.

- Re-arrange the furniture to open up the room.

- Treat yourself to some sumptuous bed linen for a fresh new look.

- Streamline to create a calm atmosphere and reduce distractions that make your eyes zing.

- Check if the curtains are making the room dark enough. The brain needs real darkness for good quality sleep – even the glow of a digital clock could affect you.

# Your notes

........................................................................

........................................................................

........................................................................

........................................................................

........................................................................

........................................................................

........................................................................

........................................................................

........................................................................

........................................................................

........................................................................

........................................................................

........................................................................

........................................................................

........................................................................

........................................................................

CHAPTER 4

**CLEAR YOUR KITCHEN**

What would it take to transform your kitchen from a messy nightmare into your dream space? A skip, a team of cleaners or simply discarding all the unused clutter? In our fast multi-tasking world the kitchen is used for a range of activities from paying bills, chatting on the phone, laundry, homework and entertaining. Even if you only microwave meals and dump the post, your goal is to make it an organised room where you enjoy spending time.

## *Activity*

## Kitchen quiz

Banish the dogs, the kids, turn off your phone and grab a few minutes to answer the kitchen clutter quiz. Score 1 point every time you answer a) and 2 points when you answer b).

**1** How often do you search for lost items like the lid for the blender?
   a) Less than once a week
   b) Most days

**2** If your mother or mother-in-law came round to visit, how long would it take you to get the kitchen to sparkle?
   a) Half an hour
   b) It's so grubby you wouldn't let anyone near it

**3** Do you clear out your fridge?
   a) Every week
   b) Can't remember the last time

**4** How many cleaning products do you have?
   a) Under 20
   b) 20+

**5** Is paperwork taking over your kitchen?
   a) There's the odd bundle
   b) Newspapers and letters are everywhere

**6** Do you chuck chipped crockery or glasses?
   a) Yes
   b) No

**7** Count the number of kitchen gadgets (like juicers) unused in the past year.
   a) 0–2
   b) 3+

**8** How would you describe your work surfaces?
   a) Clear and uncluttered
   b) Can't see the surfaces for debris

**9** Are your kitchen cupboards and drawers?
   a) Easy to use and in good order
   b) Jammed full of old junk

**Your score**

Over 12 – Take action before you qualify for *How Clean is Your House*?!

## *Activity*
## Be inspired

Now you know your clutter status, your final task for the day is to find a picture of a kitchen you love and stick it on the fridge. This will inspire you and keep you motivated.

Are you frustrated by how much food gets wasted every week? You're not alone – research reveals that up to 40 per cent of fresh food bought in the UK is chucked out. In our busy lives it's common to shop haphazardly or find ourselves tempted by the latest yoghurt drink or organic soup.

## TOP TIP

- Recipe junkies periodically buy exotic ingredients and then use a tiny amount. If you loved the dish, cook up a big batch for the freezer with the leftovers.
- Beware bargains – those tempting 'buy one, get one free' or 'three for two' offers. If your food cupboards are crammed full, they'll just clutter up your kitchen. Shop with a list and stick to it.
- Don't bulk buy organic food. It goes off more quickly so buy small quantities more often.
- Are you in a rut? Do you choose the same foods, week in week out, regardless of season or mood? Buy one new ingredient every time you shop to spice meals up. If you've never tasted papaya or sweet potato, have fun experimenting.
- Online grocery shopping is ideal if you don't have a car or have a young family. Imagine no more toddler tantrums as you fill the trolley. Another benefit is you're less likely to impulse buy.

*Activity*

# Bin fusty food and organise the rest

If you're continually running out of basics and having to dash to the shops, prepare to get your food supplies in order.

- Ditch out-of-date herbs and spices. If you hate cloves or paprika, bin them – there's no law that says you must stock a complete set.

- Drag everything out of the fridge and have a good clearout. If leftovers always end up mouldy, put that last slice of pizza on the compost straight away.

- Defrost your freezer after eating up the contents. In future defrost every three months and label and date everything you freeze.

- Empty your food cupboards and check all the sell-by dates. Take this opportunity to give the shelves a wipe over. Always put new cans and bottles at the back so you use the oldest ones first.

- Store like with like. If your tins of tomatoes or cans of tuna are together, its obvious when you need to order more.

- Question why you have 11 boxes of herbal teas going musty. Compost or use up what you have and then limit yourself to two or three opened boxes at once. Remember – less choice simplifies life!

- Match the amount of food you buy to your lifestyle. If you cook twice a week you don't need a huge weekly shop. Buying a large cabbage doesn't guarantee you're going to eat it!

CLEAR YOUR KITCHEN

51

Even mundane objects like bowls should be a pleasure to use. Adopt William Morris's philosophy: 'Have nothing in your houses that you do not know to be useful or believe to be beautiful.'

## TOP TIP

◆ Wedding presents can pose a particular hurdle. It feels ungrateful to give away the tea-set from your Aunt Sarah. But if you've never used it and have no plans to do so in the future, it's simply clutter. A common solution is to leave it at the back of the dresser and guiltily get it out when your aunt visits. The downside is that, for the rest of the year, it takes up storage space. Be brave and let it go. There's no need to offend your aunt or for her to ever know.

◆ If your kids have left home and you prefer to meet friends in restaurants, is your kitchen equipped for mass entertaining? Free yourself by donating surplus stuff. For your next party, hire wine glasses with the booze or use up paper plates you've stashed away.

*Activity*

## Dump grotty crockery and glasses

- Start by sorting your glasses. Recycle any that are chipped, ruined by the dishwasher and the tacky beer glasses. If 12 wine glasses fit comfortably into your cupboard, then keep that number.

- Repeat this process with your mugs, plates, bowls, serving dishes, and baby and toddler bottles and beakers.

- Sort your supply of storage containers. Is your kitchen full of jars, margarine cartons, picnic paraphernalia and lidless plastic containers? Hoarders are very attracted to these items and while it's definitely true that a few can be useful, you don't need to save huge stocks.

- Now move on to your 'best' china and glasses. Do they only see the light of day at celebrations? Consider using your expensive dinner service and glasses more often. The fear holding most people back is that something will break. Enjoy your things and try not to fret about normal wear and tear. Revel in drinking wine out of an elegant glass at the end of a hard day!

CLEAR YOUR KITCHEN

Kitchen clutter reflects a fantasy life – where we bake cakes, juice oranges for breakfast and host elaborate dinner parties. Freshly brewed espresso seemed such a good idea when I brought home my glamorous new coffee machine. Yet a year later, reality hit – I had only used it twice because it was time-consuming and a real effort to clean. These days I'm content with a cafetiere and a handful of useful objects like a blender, a slow cooker and a toaster.

## *Activity*

## Blitz kitchen gadgets and pans

Today's challenge is to drop the fantasy of being a domestic paragon. Instead, focus on matching the contents of your kitchen to your real life.

### Gadgets

A recent survey by the *Observer Food Magazine* found that one in four of us own five or more gadgets like juicers, ice-cream makers and sandwich makers yet we use less than a third of them. How many bulky gadgets are bunged on top of your cupboards or cluttering up your work surfaces?

Concentrate on one gadget at a time and collect up all the scattered attachments. If you haven't used it in the last year, sell it or give it to a friend. Don't plonk it in the loft or garage – that's a clutter shuffle!

### Pans

Hoarders apply the principle that you can never have enough pans and over the years amass huge collections. When they buy a new set, the old ones remain firmly in place. But what's the point? Even when entertaining you're still restricted by the number of burners on the hob.

Just hold on to good-quality pans you enjoy using. If your cast iron set feels too heavy or you haven't used your pressure cooker since college, be ruthless.

**Baking trays**

Where did all the rusting muffin trays and baking tins come from? Did you inherit these or were you once a more enthusiastic cook? Unless you love to bake, you don't need cake tins in every possible size. If most of your equipment is beyond redemption, recycle the metal at the local council tip. Don't rush out and immediately get replacements. Wait and see what you actually miss!

## Relax!

Kitchens have become a gladiatorial arena, with state-of-the-art equipment and the pressure to produce restaurant standard food for our friends. Research has shown that men are also becoming more involved in this highly competitive entertaining. Take a step back, relax and remember it's about enjoying yourself – rather than winning stars.

### TOP TIP

◆ Like a magpie are you irresistibly drawn to shiny new gadgets for your kitchen? Do you pore over catalogues or scour the high street looking for one more object to transform your home? If you can't say no, stay away from temptation while you're getting used to your uncluttered kitchen.

CLEAR YOUR KITCHEN

Kitchen drawers are like a vortex, sucking in flotsam – old keys, ancient receipts and telephone numbers alongside rusty tin openers and countless corkscrews. Hopefully there's nothing worse ... like rotting food or dead spiders!

## CASE STUDY

In one of her kitchen drawers Helen had nine pairs of oven gloves, 22 tea towels, six tea cosies, 17 champagne corks, 21 boxes of matches, 18 cab cards and more dusters than she could count. Why had she hoarded so much? She liked the feeling that she was never going to run out of anything – if one pair of oven gloves developed a hole, reinforcements were on hand. But even she had to admit that most of them were in a sorry state and overdue for the bin. Collecting champagne corks had become a unrewarding habit and it didn't hurt to dump the lot. Her tea towels were more of a sticking point – but she made a start by reducing the number to 15!

## TOP TIP

◆ Cutlery trays are good for subdividing other stuff as well as knives and forks. You can separate useful stuff like elastic bands and batteries this way. Plastic containers like ice-cream cartons also make good in-drawer storage.

# Activity

## Say goodbye to scary kitchen drawers

Imagine for a second a world where kitchen drawers open easily and everyday objects are clearly visible. This isn't an impossible dream – simply discard rubbish and use some basic organisational skills.

- Empty one drawer at a time and give it a thorough clean.

- Cutlery is functional and should be a pleasure to use. Get rid of anything that's bent or grotty. If fish knives or grapefruit spoons don't suit your lifestyle, donate them today.

- Count up similar items – you know you don't need four soup ladles or nine tin openers. Pick your favourite and let the rest go.

- Designate a specific purpose for each drawer – one for tea towels, one for cutlery and another for instruction manuals for your cooker and gadgets.

- Collect together all mystery items like keys. If you haven't identified them in two months, chuck them.

# Activity

## Check your progress

Pop into your bedroom and check out your wardrobe – is it still looking as glorious as it did a week or two ago? If not, nip any creeping clutter in the bud. A crucial concept in keeping order is never to reclutter an area – that way it's provides ongoing inspiration for current and future projects.

CLEAR YOUR KITCHEN

Now your cupboards, drawers and food supplies are in fantastic order, the final step is to tackle the remaining messy areas like the work surfaces and the cleaning products.

## *Activity* Complete the kitchen blitz

### Clear your work surfaces

● Only allow items that you use every day like teabags and the kettle to be out on the worktops. The less cluttered surfaces are, the easier they'll be to clean!

● Banish paperwork from the kitchen. Find somewhere more suitable for your bills and documents.

● Compost the row of ailing plants on your windowsill. One healthy plant will look so much better.

● Wash your dishes or load the dishwasher every day to stop the kitchen getting clogged up.

### Take stock of your cleaning products

Housework and laundry are unwelcome chores for most people. We hope in vain that a new powder or antibacterial spray will deliver us from the tedium but instead our cupboards become crammed full of cleaning materials.

● In the short term stop buying and use up what you already have.

● Use multipurpose cleaners.

● Experiment with green products like vinegar or E cloths to reduce the toxic load of chemicals in the environment.

CLEAR YOUR KITCHEN

58

## Cookery books

Glossy cookery books are so appealing that it's easy to end up with bulging bookshelves.

- Give away any duds like *100 ways with grapefruit*!

- Customise the ones you keep – add notes of when you cooked recipes and ways of improving them. It's so easy to forget this information in day-to-day life.

- Break free from cooking chilli con carne and stir-fry and make good use of your cookbooks. Resolve to try a new recipe every week.

- If you clip recipes from the paper or magazines, create a folder divided into categories like soups, puddings and vegetarian meals.

### TOP TIP

- Stand back and see if there are any other eyesores you've yet to reach. Are the tops of your cupboards groaning with miscellaneous junk? Is your noticeboard sprouting layers of paper? Are there kids' toys and carrier bags scattered around on the floor? Deal with these right away!

- Dust and grease are a tell-tale sign that something is clutter. Try and remember the last time you used grubby neglected items. If you're unlikely to need them again, it's time to part company.

CLEAR YOUR KITCHEN

Another room complete – well done! The kitchen is a particular challenge to keep gleaming because of the heavy traffic it attracts. But you can do it by establishing a few basic routines and curbing your hoarding habits.

## Reward

Treat yourself to a spring clean from a local firm as a reward for all your effort. It's so much simpler to stay on top of jobs if you start off with a sparkling clean kitchen.

*Activity*

## Keep your kitchen clutter free

Kitchen storage solutions are constantly evolving – check out a design shop today or flick though a magazine for inspiration.

### Shopping for supplies

Think of your kitchen as a stock room for domestic supplies. You should know exactly what's in store and create a system for reordering things. Always have a shopping list on the go. As soon as you open the last bottle of bleach or olive oil, add it to the list. If you shop online, you could print off your list from the internet and stick it on the side of the fridge so you can highlight items as they need replacing.

### Bad habits alert!

- Don't bring home packets of sugar, plastic spoons, serviettes and packets of matches from cafés.

- Stop littering your work surfaces with loose change. Use a container to hold coins instead.

- Stop overbuying cut-price food. Even if it's cheap, your cupboards will end up bulging with all the bargains. Offers come around every week so you're unlikely to miss out!

- Resist buying complicated gizmos to stone cherries or pare lemons.

- Don't dump rubbish or unopened letters into kitchen drawers. This head-in-the-sand approach will cause trouble in the long term.

CLEAR YOUR KITCHEN

# Your notes

........................................................

........................................................

........................................................

........................................................

........................................................

........................................................

........................................................

........................................................

........................................................

........................................................

........................................................

........................................................

........................................................

........................................................

........................................................

........................................................

........................................................

CHAPTER

# LIBERATE YOUR
# LIVING SPACE

Living rooms are where we entertain, watch TV, chat on the phone, where our kids play and where we curl up to unwind with a glass of wine. Yet this room is often jam-packed with oversized furniture and walls dripping with pictures. Large collections of books and DVDs fill the space. Newspapers coat every surface and dusty ornaments are dotted everywhere. Hardly an alluring environment, is it?

## TOP TIP

To gain some perspective on the living room, take photos from different angles. Visit a coffee shop and lay out your photos on the table. Imagine you're viewing the room for the first time – what would you revamp? How would you create more space?

## The big stuff

Furniture can be clutter for two reasons:

◆ You have too much to fit comfortably into the room. Perhaps your last home had more generous proportions or you've moved in with your partner and crammed both your sofas in.
◆ Your tastes have altered and that patterned rug looks garish to you now.

Spend a few minutes daydreaming about what can be done to improve the flow and feel of your living room. Perhaps the layout needs rearranging or you could lose an extra armchair?

*Activity*

## Living room clutter quiz

Calculate the chaos quota by taking the living room clutter quiz. Score 1 for each statement you agree with:

1   I rarely invite friends round – I'm too ashamed of the mess.

2   I can never sit on the sofa without clearing bits and pieces off first.

3   The living room floor is covered in junk.

4   I find the clutter depressing when I sit down in the evenings.

5   Are any of the following crowding the room (score 1 for each)?
   ● kids' toys
   ● work projects
   ● piles of newspapers
   ● magazines more than three months old
   ● CDs/DVDs, computer games out of their cover
   ● dog chews and cat toys
   ● mounds of ironing
   ● abandoned craft projects
   ● jackets or discarded bags
   ● stuff behind the sofa (like rolls of wallpaper)
   ● a selection of sorry-looking plants
   ● too much furniture.

**Your score**

Under 3: The living room is pretty clutter free.
4–9: Mess is taking over.
10–16: Clutter is winning – time to reclaim your room!

LIBERATE YOUR LIVING SPACE

Decorative touches often evolve haphazardly – we start with one house plant … six months later we've got a jungle. A couple of framed photos rapidly expand into a picture gallery. Suddenly, instead of enhancing the room, accessories are overwhelming it.

## *Activity*

## Weed out your accessories

Look closely at the ornaments in the living room. You should be using them to create sensational surroundings. Just like a shop window, you can experiment with new arrangements to restyle the room.

### Photos

Once photos make it into the frame, they seem to stay there forever. Choose more recent shots or stack a few photos in the frame so you can rotate them easily.

### Plants

A vibrant plant or two is fine but yellowing ones in the fireplace looks awful. Watch out too for fresh flowers that are wilting and dried flowers that are more dust-trap than dazzling!

## Knick-knacks

Is every available table, shelf and window sill festooned with candle sticks, souvenirs, swimming trophies and bowls of pot pourri? Does it feel cosy or more like you've wandered into a junk shop? Say farewell to dull ornaments and store sentimental items you no longer want on show.

## Paintings and prints

Are the walls a mishmash of different paintings and prints? Tastes evolve and change – the poster you chose as a student won't work when you're 40. Make sure you love all your pictures and they aren't overcrowding the walls.

## Soft furnishings

Cushions and throws can really enhance a room – especially if you've got an ageing sofa. On the other hand, too many makes sitting on the sofa a challenge! Give away the superfluous ones today.

Upmarket home-cinema systems and deluxe flat screen TVs are now the latest trend. We're in a period of accelerated change when conventional TV is being replaced by digital and the number of channels is ever-growing. Videos are old hat now that DVDs are here.

## Scary fact

On average, UK households watch more than 3.5 hours of TV a day compared to a European average of 3 hours and a US average of 4.5 hours. It's worrying how many negative reports there are of childhood obesity and insomnia linked to long hours of TV watching.

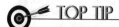 TOP TIP

♦ Even if you're a big fan of TV, why not declare Sunday a no TV day, which makes a relaxing wrap-up to the weekend.

♦ If you're having problems finding time every day to declutter, just watching half an hour less TV would give you that space. Give it a try.

## Do

♦ Differentiate between one-watch films and others you'll want to keep and view again and again.

♦ Rent don't buy. As well as your local rental shop, there are a number of online schemes, like the ones run by Amazon and Tesco, where you can rent DVDs by post.

♦ Now everyone is switching to DVDs, charity shops are full of videos. For a couple of quid you can buy a film or a kids' cartoon. Once you're done, take it back to the charity shop – the charity benefits twice over and you stay clutter free.

♦ Reunite DVDs with their covers to prevent damage. If one gets lost, buy a replacement cover and label it.

♦ Get attractive storage for your collection. Ideally this would be concealed storage like a specially designed shelving unit.

LIBERATE YOUR LIVING SPACE

*Activity*

# Thin out your collections

Most hoarders have stacks of videos and DVDs that urgently need a thorough sort out.

## Videos

Do you still own every *Thomas the Tank Engine* video even though your kids are teenagers? Do your exercise videos date back to Jane Fonda and Mr Motivator? Are you reluctant to write off films like *Dirty Dancing* or *Mad Max* that you haven't watched in years? Either dust them off and watch them or give them away today.

Decide on a policy for videos. I'm slowly replacing my small video library of feel-good films with the DVD versions.

## DVDs

Do you rush out the minute a new film is released on DVD and buy it at full price? Not only is this expensive, but if the film's boring you're left with a DVD you don't want. Wait a bit to see if the film has lasting appeal before buying.

In theory, new technologies like MP3 players mean our music collections will take up a tiny amount of space in our homes. But there's nothing quite like vinyl or owning a CD, complete with lyrics and cover notes.

*Activity*

## Fine-tune your music collections

### Tapes and cassettes

Many people cling on to tapes long after they've switched to CDs. Start playing old favourites like Wham or Culture Club or pass them on to a charity shop.

Portable CD players rarely include a cassette deck now, which reflects how tapes have fallen out of favour. After all, who wants to spend time unravelling a chewed-up tape with a pencil when you could enjoy a track on your i-Pod or CD?

If you decide to ditch all your tapes, do give away any associated equipment like storage racks and personal stereos.

### Records

LPs and singles are either pure clutter or true treasure. Hoarders can be in total chaos apart from an immaculately alphabetised vinyl collection!

People seem to have got rid of cumbersome old record players but held on to the LPs. Manufacturers have cottoned on to this and it's easy to buy an inexpensive, slimline record player that will plug into your CD system. Time to choose – either get something to play records on or let them go.

## CDs

If you have a splurge and buy lots of CDs at once, you might find that they sit around for weeks, neglected. Whereas if you buy one at time, you're more likely to listen to each one thoroughly.

Have you got lots of CDs you've barely listened to or some still in their wrappers? Sell or give away expendable ones and then put the rest into categories that make sense to you like jazz, or film scores.

### Freebies

There seem to be a rash of giveaway CDs with magazines and newspapers. I love getting them, but I usually listen to them a couple of times, then pass them on. Make sure they don't clutter up your home!

### Storage

CDs work well in open racks that are easy to access. Wall storage is always an excellent solution for saving space. There are brilliantly designed products on the market so have fun choosing! It helps to have a rough idea of the number of CDs you want to house so you select one that's big enough as well as good looking.

Staying on top of paper is a constant battle. I'm pretty determined, but if I didn't gather newspapers for recycling every day, my living room would soon be awash.

## *Activity*

## Purge the living room of its paper trail

Be merciless and blitz newspapers, magazines, catalogues and circulars quickly and unemotionally. If you're a paper hoarder you're going to find this tough but think how great the room will look when you've finished.

- Remember, it's more important to restore balance to your living room than to catch up on back numbers.

- Very few people have the time to thoroughly read newspapers every day – particularly the weekend ones with all their supplements.

- Old papers are old news.

- Junk mail is called that for a good reason.

- You won't be missing out on fascinating stories and exciting holiday offers by throwing things away. They'll keep coming.

- Hanging on to catalogues in case you might be interested in future is hoarding. Only save those you use regularly. Although you may not even need to do this as there are plenty of online catalogues.

- This isn't an excuse to sit for half an hour with your feet up reading month-old news stories!

LIBERATE YOUR LIVING SPACE

**TOP TIP**

- Make a decision never to keep any newspapers more than a week old.
- Only buy a paper when you have time to enjoy it.
- Put magazines in an accessible rack or basket so you can grab one on your way to work. If you haven't looked at them in a month's time, recycle them. In the meantime, don't buy any more to add to the pile.
- Cancel subscriptions to magazines that never make it out of the plastic wrapper. This saves time and money.
- Only buy this month's magazine when you've finished with and decluttered last month's.

Books hold a special place in many people's hearts. The mantra that many book lovers adopt is 'a book is for life and never to be parted with'. But if you're a prolific reader, this will soon lead to sagging shelves and overloaded bookcases. Once you run out of space, paperbacks will end up piled on the floor or carted off to the loft.

## CASE STUDY

Sheila felt her books were central to her identity and she never parted with a single one. As a result, her collection was so large that it spilled into the garage. When she finally got round to sorting it out, all the books were mouldy and disintegrating. For a bookworm like Sheila this was heartbreaking. She realised that it would have been so much better to pass them on years ago!

## TOP TIP

- Don't automatically slip a newly read book onto your shelves. Consider first whether you're likely to read it again in the future.
- Never hoard classics because they look good on the shelves – it doesn't make sense if you're not a fan of Charles Dickens or Jane Austen.
- Books for many people equal knowledge. But don't fall into the trap of keeping a large library just to impress other people with your learning!
- Coffee-table books look gorgeous and make glossy presents. The trouble is they rarely get opened after the first browse. Don't hold on to these as decorative items – declutter them today.

# *Activity*
## Edit your book collection

Aim to bring order to your collection so you can find books easily.

- Differentiate between important books you want to reread and one-off reads like chick-lit or thrillers that you can happily give away to friends, family or the local charity shop or Oxfam bookshop.

- Separate out unread fiction. Stack it horizontally as a visual reminder.

- Limit how many books you have on the go at any one time. Otherwise you end up with several half-read books. Challenge the belief that every book should be read from cover to cover – ditch a dull novel part way through. Life's too short to waste on duds when there are so many great stories to read!

- Only keep current reference books. Information is always changing so recycle out-of-date ones.

- Give kids' books to nurseries or school libraries, or to a friend with younger children.

- Join your local library – that way you have to return your books.

Open-plan living means that many of us don't have separate dining rooms anymore. Kitchen diners or a knocked-through lounge with a dining area are increasingly popular. Family meals have been replaced by grazing, conflicting timetables and eating on our laps in front of the TV.

*Activity*

## Create a pleasant space for sociable dining

Festive get-togethers may be the only time we sweep all the junk off the dining table. But would you share meals with family or friends more if the table was tidy?

- Make better use of your dining area by scheduling at least one meal at the table every week. That way you'll have the incentive to keep it clear.

- Get a box and scoop off all the clutter on the table.

- Decide what activities will happen here in future – can craft projects and your kids' homework be done anywhere else? If this is the only option, make sure that the table's decluttered daily and that there's enough storage nearby for any related items.

- Make a decision whether to use this as an area for a computer or for handling paperwork. Just because it's been used this way in the past doesn't mean it's set in stone. If you work here sometimes or pay your bills at the table, find an attractive wooden filing cabinet that won't look out of place in your dining room.

- Find new places for all the homeless clutter that's accumulated here.

- Don't put anything back on the table except a beautiful bowl of fruit.

**Open up the space**

If you don't use the dining table very often, then it's taking up a lot of room for little return. It's a case of use it or lose it. You could exchange your large table for a fold-away model and fold-up chairs.

**Sideboard**

- Streamline the numerous tablecloths and napkins you never use. Who has the time to starch table linen these days?

- If you store fine china and glasses in the dining room, look back to the tips on Day 23.

- Is your wedding list coming back to haunt you? Do you still believe that you need avocado bowls, corn-on-the-cob dishes and six kinds of wine glasses? If your entertaining style is more casual now, then let superfluous china go.

Now that you've blitzed the paper, the ornaments, the books, DVDs and music, your living space should be looking wonderful. A few final steps will heighten the harmonious atmosphere.

## TOP TIP

It's a living room so it doesn't have to be immaculate 100 per cent of the time. Don't whisk away a cup of coffee the second it's finished. Relax! Instead, spend five minutes a day picking up stray items before they become a permanent feature. Make this a routine – I usually do it first thing but others prefer to speed tidy after the kids have gone to bed.

*Activity*

# Work on the outstanding clutter

Perch on the sofa and see if you can spot any congested areas. Has your recently cleared mantelpiece suddenly sprouted bits of Lego and a sprinkling of unopened mail?

- If there are loads of kids' toys, rotate them with those stored in the bedroom. Provide adequate storage so your kids have somewhere to put things away in the evening. Use dual-purpose furniture like a trunk that can double as a coffee table.

- If you continue to feel cramped by your possessions, lose a couple more plants, cushions or even a lamp.

- Whenever old habits start to emerge, like holding on to last week's newspapers, or if debris is piling up on the floor, take action immediately.

- Treat yourself to a bunch of flowers to celebrate successfully creating a lovely living space. Then invite friends round to marvel at the transformation.

LIBERATE YOUR LIVING SPACE

# Your notes

CHAPTER

6

# CREATE SPACE IN YOUR HALL AND BATHROOM

When you open your front door, do you see a dumping ground for bags, newspapers and scattered shoes? Do you drop yet more stuff and scuttle past into a more relaxing room? It doesn't need to be this way! With determined decluttering and decent storage, it can be a welcoming spot in its own right.

## *Activity*

## Clear the hall and stairs to improve the energy flow

Your aim is to thoroughly clear the hallway and to shift all the junk that's accumulated on the stairs.

### The stairs

Staircases aren't a storage area, although many people use them that way. It looks messy and it can be a serious safety hazard. Start by picking up any stray objects that are obstructing the stairs and take them to where they belong.

The ongoing challenge with the stairs is to find an effective way to deal with things on the way up or down. Stair baskets are a good solution as long as you don't fill them up permanently with property magazines and stray socks.

### Cloakrooms

If you have a ground floor cloakroom, are you littering it with discarded shoes, outgrown jackets, endless plants and a jumble of quirky books? Does this work for you or would you prefer a more sophisticated look?

Once you've thinned out the cloakroom clutter, you'll see the decorative potential of this room much more clearly.

**Under-stair cupboards**

These can be incredibly useful storage for your vacuum cleaner, the tool box and household supplies like light bulbs. But they also seem to attract rubbish like defunct irons and holey wellington boots. Size up the situation before you empty everything out and start again. Do you need to have a real blitz just on this area?

Make sure you have suitable lighting or it will be impossible to keep this cupboard well-ordered. You could simply add a clip-on light.

Put seasonal equipment like your picnic set at the back and frequently used items like your torch near the front.

## TOP TIP

◆ Check the lighting is bright enough in the hallway. A dingy space lit by a 40-watt bulb will encourage clutter.
◆ Make sure there are enough hooks for everyone to hang their coats and bags. Young children need these at their own height so they have no excuse for chucking their belongings on the floor.
◆ A shoe cupboard or rack can accommodate everyday shoes. But do take the overflow back to bedrooms on a regular basis.
◆ Use your hall table for outgoing post or a DVD that needs returning. Don't let circulars and free newspapers spoil this useful spot.

'You only have one chance to make a first impression.'
Anonymous

CREATE SPACE IN YOUR HALL AND BATHROOM

Bathrooms can be luxurious ensuite havens or small, overcrowded rooms for all the family. If yours is more soggy towels than sanctuary, then make a start today.

## Activity

## Create a relaxing, uncluttered bathroom

### Clear out your bathroom cabinet

- Empty the cabinet and give it a speed clean.

- List first-aid items that need replacing.

- Take out-of-date medicines to the pharmacy for safe disposal.

- Throw out anything that's gungy or leaking.

- Give away unopened beauty or grooming products that were misguided buys or unwanted gifts.

- Store like with like – so all painkillers are together and easy to find.

- Use a permanent marker to date new bottles like suntan lotion. That way you'll know when to replace them.

- Make it a routine to sort out your bathroom cabinet every six months.

### Towels

- In a hotel it's lovely to have a fresh towel every day, but at home, who's going to wash them! Change them every few days – that way you'll only need two to three bath towels per person. Reserve a handful of guest towels as well.

- Beach towels can double up for the gym or for your kids' swimming lessons.

- Colour code towels so one person has white, another blue and so on. That way, you'll never get them mixed up.

- Recycle any scratchy or threadbare towels today.

- Displaying clean folded towels looks great in catalogues but if yours never look as pristine, store them in the linen cupboard.

## The bin

Use a pedal bin instead of the floor for bottles, toilet roll innards and other rubbish. I often see bathrooms with pointless junk like empty shampoo and shower gel bottles around the bath. Why not recycle them right away?

## Papers and books

The world divides into those who read in the bathroom and those who don't. The toilet floor looks awful strewn with ancient newspapers and fading magazines. If you like reading material in the bathroom, install either a shelf or a basket to hold everything. Have a regular clearout and update your magazines.

## Cleaning supplies

Most bathrooms have a cupboard under the sink suitable for cleaning supplies. Make sure this locks if you have young children. Follow the guidelines on Day 26 to organise your stock. Finally, don't bulk buy toilet rolls and bleach if you've nowhere to store them.

'There's no need to go to India or anywhere else to find peace. You will find that deep place of silence right in your room, your garden or even your bathtub.' Elisabeth Kubler-Ross, psychiatrist

CREATE SPACE IN YOUR HALL AND BATHROOM

Last time you had a bath, was it a relaxing, uplifting experience or were you staring at plastic ducks, missing tiles and overflowing laundry? You deserve better. Recall the most relaxing bathroom you've ever been in and recreate that peaceful atmosphere at home.

## Successful storage

Consider over-the-door hooks, vertical towel rails, a bigger bathroom cabinet or a free-standing unit for your soaps and towels. Invest in a new-generation laundry basket with separate compartments for whites and coloured clothes. But if space is tight, use a drawstring laundry bag that you can hang on the back of the bathroom door.

'I can't think of any sorrow in the world that a hot bath wouldn't help, just a little bit.' Susan Glaspell, playwright and author

 TOP TIP

In future treat yourself to one or two gorgeous pampering products rather than the entire contents of the chemist's shelves.

*Activity*

# Create a spa ambience in your bathroom

Concentrate on completing the transformation you began yesterday.

**Do**

- Finish up the dregs in bottles of bubble bath and conditioner. Be strict with yourself – don't buy or open any new ones until you've used everything up.

- Blitz your washing over the next few days to unclog your laundry basket.

- If your bathroom surfaces are clutter free, then it'll be a doddle to keep them sparkling clean!

**Don't**

- Don't overfill your bathroom with plants, shells, candles and postcards.

- Don't let kids' toys dominate this space. Store them in a plastic container or mesh net that can be hung up.

- Unfinished DIY can spoil the bathroom. If yours is in a state of disrepair, make a note of jobs that need attention and either schedule in time yourself or arrange for outside help.

CREATE SPACE IN YOUR HALL AND BATHROOM

# Your notes

# CHAPTER 7

## SPRUCE UP YOUR SPARE ROOM

When you first saw your home did you imagine turning the spare room into a craft room, a cosy place to welcome guests or the office you've always dreamed of? You probably didn't think it would be a great junk room!

## CASE STUDY

Gavin's spare room was typical of many others – it had become so overrun with clutter that he could barely squeeze the door open, let alone get in. His dream was to create a studio where he could write and record music. With this firmly in mind, he was ruthless. Out went his rugby kit, the dinner service he never used, bundles of magazines and a lifetime's worth of cards. A carpenter then designed custom-built storage for his LPs and other music collections. The highest cupboards held memorabilia like family cinefilms and photo albums. He loves his new studio but says he gets the odd withdrawal when he just wants to dump something in there!

## Motivate yourself

Calculate how much money you're paying in rent or mortgage each month for a room full of junk. It's an expensive way to store empty shoe boxes and old copies of the *Radio Times*. Bear this figure in mind and it will bolster your determination to make the best possible use of the space.

*Activity*

## Redefine your spare room

Visualise your spare room transformed into your ideal space. What activities would be going on here and who would be using it? Before you can achieve this dream, you'll need to deal with all the assorted oddments that have washed up here. Spare rooms attract things that should have been scrapped years ago, so this is one space where you can afford to be ruthless with useless possessions.

**Get cracking**

- Tackle the floor first – the minute it's cleared, you're going to feel a lot more positive about the whole project.

- Grab a large bin liner and chuck any obvious garbage that's covering up the carpet – broken lampshades, dried-out cosmetics, faulty electric blankets, unused diaries from five years ago. You get the picture. Approach your spare room like an archaeological dig – today you're taking the grottiest layer off first.

- At this stage use a box to temporarily stash things you want to keep. We'll be looking at some nifty storage ideas in a couple of days.

'To accomplish great things, we must dream as well as act.'
Anatole France, French novelist

SPRUCE UP YOUR SPARE ROOM

Spare rooms have a magnetic attraction for hoarders. Here's a hidey hole where all sorts of flotsam and jetsam can be stashed away for years. Now you've finally opened up the door, don't be discouraged by the magnitude of the task. Take things one step at a time and you'll succeed in jettisoning carloads of clutter.

## Trash or treasure?

I'm sure there are many long-forgotten and abandoned objects in your spare room. Even if your tea or coffee maker is an old friend, you've lived without it for years so you probably won't notice it when it's left the house. Don't let sentiment overpower your decision-making. Even though you had a fantastic trip to Florida, don't hang on to every table serviette or box of matches you collected!

## *Activity*

### Continue digging through the clutter

Yesterday you made a flying start on the spare room. Today, carry on with this challenging area.

### Paperwork

Don't get bogged down in sorting out individual pieces of paper at this stage as it's one of the most laborious jobs. Temporarily put all paperwork into a plastic crate. But do recycle any old magazines, brochures, catalogues or newspapers you come across straight away. Paperwork will be dealt with in detail in Chapter 12.

### Cardboard boxes

New appliances come with a lot of packaging. Ideally you'd keep the box while the product is under guarantee. Of course if you have a loft, this is no sweat – but if you live in a ground-floor flat, your spare room's soon going to be taken over by these monstrosities. Flatten them out and stick them behind a cupboard or under the bed. But if you don't have space, get rid of the boxes and recycle the cardboard.

### Clothes storage

Spare rooms often house an overflow wardrobe. Use it for out-of-season clothing and special-occasion outfits. But don't hang on to dated jackets and coats simply because you have extra room. You're bound to be able to make better use of the space.

### Fabrics

Redundant sets of curtains, tablecloths and napkins tend to migrate to the spare room. If you don't need them or use them, give them away today.

### Craft and DIY projects

Creative hoarders love to acquire bits and bobs for making cards, for sewing, or as contributions to DIY projects. Again, box these up and we'll deal with them on Day 61.

## TOP TIP

If your spare room's a real nightmare, put aside a couple more days for the decluttering task. If you feel progress is slow-going, deliver the full bags to charity – that way you'll see the clear space that's emerging.

SPRUCE UP YOUR SPARE ROOM

Obviously if you're creating a home office you'll want good storage for your paperwork. Similarly, if it's going to be a play room, you'll need containers for the toys and games.

*Activity*

## Maximise the storage potential of the spare room

- Save space on beds. If your spare room is doubling up as an office and guest room, consider replacing your bulky double bed with a wall bed or sofa bed. The latest blow-up beds are a practical option too. They're quick to inflate and fold away to almost nothing. They're brilliant, too, for kids' sleepovers.

- Optimise your wall space. Floor-to-ceiling fitted wardrobes or cupboards provide fantastic storage. Imagine having room for your winter coats, party clothes, back copies of your tax returns and other basics.

- Transparent plastic containers make flexible storage for anything from kids' toys to pieces of fabric,

- Vacuum pack out-of-season clothing or spare duvets so they take up less space.

- Don't reclutter. Never again chuck something into this room 'just for now' or use the sofa bed as a hangout for laundry.

- Be selective about what to store in your spare room. Remember that one definition of clutter is having too many things for the space. Bear this in mind whenever you're hanging on to something unimportant.

## Rename it

It's no longer the junk room or spare room but the office, study, guest room or play room. Renaming it will help you take ownership of it and maximise its potential.

# Your notes

........................................................................................

........................................................................................

........................................................................................

........................................................................................

........................................................................................

........................................................................................

........................................................................................

........................................................................................

........................................................................................

........................................................................................

........................................................................................

........................................................................................

........................................................................................

........................................................................................

........................................................................................

........................................................................................

# CHAPTER 8

## SORT THE
## SCARY AREAS

The activities in this chapter are going to take time and effort. They aren't jobs that you can finish in 30 minutes. Either allocate a day or the whole weekend to attack the problem zone in one big blitz. If that's too daunting, break each area down into manageable tasks that can fit into your daily routine.

## TOP TIP

- Don't panic. If it feels like opening Pandora's box, then take it at your own pace. Expect it to be emotional and to trigger many memories.
- If you've shoved things in randomly, it'll be a nightmare to find the family tent or the floor sander. Dedicate a few minutes to drawing up a floor plan for the optimum storage layout.
- When you buy a new laptop, don't automatically stow the old one in the loft. Do you honestly think you'll use it again in three years? It would be so much better to pass it on while it's still of use to somebody.
- Don't feel you have to fill every centimetre of space. My mum cleared out her loft years ago and it's totally empty. It makes her feel good, having that uncluttered expanse above her home.

'You will tend to worry more about the future than other people, as if there are problems hanging over you, ready to drop at any time!' Karen Kingston, a leading Feng Shui expert, on storing clutter in the attic

SORT THE SCARY AREAS

*Activity*

## Make the best use of the loft and cellar

If you have a loft and a cellar, treat these as two separate projects.

Most people find the prospect overwhelming and wait until they're forced to take action when moving home, converting the loft or a pipe bursts in the cellar. Be brave and make a start today.

If you have a floored loft or a cellar with enough headroom, then sort things out in situ. But if you have to bring the boxes out, then tackle one at a time.

- Lofts tend to be used for jumble that should never have been stored, like Betamax video recorders and the fading carpet from your old home. Treat the junk with the respect it deserves and bin or recycle it.

- Historical items like childhood toys often languish unloved in lofts. Ask yourself why, if they're so precious, you stash them out of sight. Be choosy and only keep significant mementos from your past.

- Organise storage in the loft and make sure boxes are labelled on all sides for easy reading. Store everything in dust- and insect-proof containers. Lofts suffer from extreme temperatures – cold in the winter, hot in the summer, so fragile china may get damaged. In a cellar, protect against damp by using plastic boxes with lids.

SORT THE SCARY AREAS

Until recently, sheds were seen as a traditional refuge for men to escape domestic life and potter around in peace and quiet. But recent research shows that, in the 21st century, 40 per cent of women also see the shed as a place to do their own thing. These days sheds contain home cinemas, office space, meditation rooms or even a bar!

## Upgrade your shed

If the shed roof is leaking and the woodlice have taken up residence, why not treat yourself to a new one? Did you know that people in the UK bought 1.5 million sheds in 2004? This reflects the growing awareness that the simple garden shed is a flexible space that can be used for much more than storage.

 TOP TIP

- ◆ In future avoid a 'chuck and run' approach – opening the door and flinging things in the shed without any thought or planning.
- ◆ Don't assume your garden is too small for a shed. There are mini-sheds available for storing basic tools.
- ◆ If your shed is getting old, remove anything that's vulnerable to damp or mould like fabrics.

# Activity

## Overhaul your garden shed

Let's assume that your garden shed is of the more traditional nature – full of rusting cans of paint, tools, ripped deckchairs, bicycle parts, carpet tiles and a lifetime's supply of plant pots.

- On a day with a promising weather forecast, throw caution to the wind and empty out the entire shed. The spiders won't thank you but give the whole area a good sweep out and clean the windows. Then only replace essential items.

- Or, if you want to approach the shed in bite-size chunks, sort the paint today and move on to the pots tomorrow.

**Do**

- Decide whether the shed has potential for more than storage. Is the junk masking the opportunity for this to be a valuable workspace? If so, what activities would you like to use the shed for?

- Recycle paint and ensure that toxic chemicals like weed killer are disposed of safely. Your local council should be able to advise you.

- Check that all your gardening tools are in good shape. Get shears sharpened and your lawnmower serviced annually. Oil blades after use to avoid rusting.

- Keep the floor uncluttered – use inexpensive metal shelving units from DIY shops and wall hooks for hanging tools.

- If you've got expensive equipment in your shed, make sure you have a strong padlock.

SORT THE SCARY AREAS

'Only in America do we leave cars worth thousands of dollars in the driveway and leave useless things and junk in boxes in the garage.' Anonymous

These days this strange attitude isn't just evident in America. It's incredibly common to move home and shunt boxes that have been unopened for many years – from one garage to another.

*Activity*

## Claim back your garage from the garbage

When did you last park your car in the garage? Is this clutter epidemic also affecting the garages of your family, friends and neighbours?

**Do**

- Survey the scale of the challenge. Do you need a friend to help you handle the sheer volume of stuff? Will you need a skip or the council to collect an old dishwasher? Plan ahead before you start hauling boxes out onto the drive.

- Aim for a well-regulated garage, making full use of the wall space with shelving and hooks.

- Restrict storage to your car, bicycles, paint or chemicals that you don't want in the house and seasonal kit like fabric sun-loungers.

- If you must store something temporarily, put the date and list of contents on the box.

- Leave room to walk around. You don't need to fill it to capacity.

- Allocate a day annually for a garage spring clean.

**TOP TIP**

- Stop viewing your garage as a place to dump stuff 'for the time being'. If you're never going to use that rug, find it a better home today.
- Control 'useful' collections like jam jars, bits of wood or biscuit tins. Recycle the surplus right away.

## Your car is not a mobile junk heap

Next time you drive your car, imagine someone you want to impress needs a lift. Would you feel embarrassed or be too busy scrabbling for the papers, coffee cups, crisp packets, petrol receipts and all the other trash?

Normally we hide our mess behind closed doors – in bedrooms and spare rooms. But when it comes to the car, unless you're in a limo with darkened windows, it's there for everyone to see. So do make clearing your car part of your regular routine. Remove rubbish daily and don't leave valuables or personal information around to tempt thieves.

Only keep specific things that belong in your car and that you actually use, like road maps. If you never listen to the Duran Duran cassette, or the Love compilation CD that cost £3.99 at the service station, then give them to charity.

Enjoy the feeling of driving around in a comfortable, clutter-free car. Reward yourself with a car valet to celebrate your achievements!

SORT THE SCARY AREAS

You don't need a rusting car in your driveway to create a cluttered impression. The front garden frames your house and it's a creative challenge to make this area attractive in spite of the wheelie bins and recycling boxes.

*Activity*

## Open up your outdoor space

- Pick up any litter that blows in to your front garden – otherwise you'll find that it attracts lager cans and other garbage.

- Arrange several decorative pots near the front door. This will create a welcoming first impression and kerbside appeal if you're selling your home.

- Resist the temptation to overcrowd your balcony or roof terrace. It's not a competition to see how many plants fit on it, rather a spot to unwind. Enjoy growing a herb garden for fragrance and to spice up your cooking.

'He who plants a garden plants happiness.' Proverb

### TOP TIP

- Don't let relics from your previous hoarding spoil your garden. Call the council to take away rotten garden furniture and broken lawn mowers.
- Be careful about leaving kids' toys out in bad weather. I had a client who spent a fortune on doll's prams and then left them out all winter to fall apart!
- Avoid buying garden furniture that isn't weatherproof – not many of us have room to store it in the garage or shed over winter.
- Never leave tools and empty pots lying around. Straighten up at the end of each gardening session.
- Neglected hanging baskets with dying flowers look miserable, so compost them and refill the baskets with healthy plants.
- Don't go overboard when you visit the garden centre or sit down with the latest catalogues. Where are you going to plant another apple tree or hebe? Do you really need a seventh watering can to add to your stockpile?

Ten years ago there were 30 self-storage warehouses in the UK and now there are 300. So what's going on? It seem that the growth of these units is a response to the cluttered age we live in. They used to be temporary solutions during a move, but now they take up the overflow from our homes.

## *Activity*

## Is self-storage an expensive home for clutter?

If you're currently using a self-storage unit, ask yourself:

- What are you storing in there? Is it tat or treasure?

- Do you even know what's in most of the boxes?

- Are you just delaying the moment you have to deal with something or let it go?

- How much is it costing you to store things you'll probably never use again?

## Good reasons to rent one

Self-storage units are ideal for short-term use during stressful times such as:

◆ moving house
◆ following a divorce or bereavement
◆ if you're renting out your home for a short period.

If you live in a tiny apartment and space is at a premium, a storage unit may work out cheaper than moving in the medium term. Use it selectively to store seasonal items like cool boxes or holiday gear.

Before you rent a unit, think long and hard about why you're holding on to things. Letting go will free you up to spend your money on something more enjoyable.

## Sorting out units you currently rent

Some hoarders have multiple units on the go, each one piled high with totally useless trash. My old neighbour used to rent four garages, simply to store broken washing machines, car parts and endless junk just in case it came in useful!

## Do

◆ Make a trip to the unit when you've got a free morning, armed with bags for the charity shop and boxes for recycling and rubbish.
◆ Be hard-hearted – remember you've lived perfectly well without this stuff for months if not years. Ask yourself if you've missed it.
◆ Label boxes so you can lay your hands on things quickly. If you've been storing things haphazardly, it's going to be frustrating finding your electric fan or your summer clothes.
◆ Be discriminating about what you store in future and never shunt junk here because it's too difficult to part with.

SORT THE SCARY AREAS

# Your notes

........................................................................................

........................................................................................

........................................................................................

........................................................................................

........................................................................................

........................................................................................

........................................................................................

........................................................................................

........................................................................................

........................................................................................

........................................................................................

........................................................................................

........................................................................................

........................................................................................

........................................................................................

# CHAPTER 9

# ENCOURAGE OTHERS
# IN YOUR HOUSEHOLD

It's easy to get frustrated with people we live with and to blame them for the muddle and mayhem at home. Everyone has their own annoying quirks and the ability to blank out particular eyesores. My husband Nick's speciality is leaving his shoes in little clumps by the sofa!

If you live alone, your task is simpler – but the downside is it can only be those pesky clutter fairies that mess the place up. Check out Day 51 if you have pets.

## *Activity*

# Involve household members

The focus so far has been on your own possessions, but now it's time to involve the people you live with. You're going to face an uphill struggle if you live with a resistant hoarder, teenagers or flatmates who believe domestic matters interfere with drinking or TV!

It's important to decide your strategy in advance so you can get others on board. Reflect on how they've reacted so far to your decluttering successes. Have they been curious, impressed or not even noticed? Has there been any sabotage? People close to you can be unsettled by change and try to undermine you.

### What works

- Get together with others in your household in a non-threatening way over a drink or a meal.

- Accept that if they're comfortable with the status quo, they may not be motivated initially. Allow them time to warm to the idea of a more orderly home.

ENCOURAGE OTHERS IN YOUR HOUSEHOLD

- Plan rewards and incentives. For kids, it could be a trip to the cinema with a friend when they've sorted out their toys. Or having their room redecorated if they can keep it tidy for a few weeks. For your partner, try a head massage or a night out!

- Lead by example. Without being evangelical, model how great your co-ordinated wardrobe or clear desk feels.

- Agree on clutter-free zones like the living room and kitchen. In return, teenagers' bedrooms or your spouse's study are their own creative space as long as they don't overstep health and safety boundaries!

**What doesn't work**

- Nagging or lecturing.

- Chucking out other people's things without their permission.

- Not respecting the right of others to make decisions about their own belongings, even if you don't agree.

- Unrealistic expectations of an overnight dramatic personality change. Hoarding is a habit that disappears slowly over time.

'A new idea is delicate. It can be killed by a sneer or a yawn; it can be stabbed to death by a joke or worried to death by a frown on the right person's brow.' Charles Brower, US advertising executive

ENCOURAGE OTHERS IN YOUR HOUSEHOLD

Your goal today is to diffuse some of the tension that's built up with your partner about clutter and disorder. A popular myth is that women are dedicated to domesticity and that men are slobs who wouldn't notice being knee-deep in junk. Even in the 21st century, women are under more pressure to take responsibility for household matters.

But there are plenty of tidy men tearing their hair out because they live with a woman who takes up 90 per cent of the wardrobe and still goes shopping day and night. Same-sex couples also bicker over who is the biggest culprit when it comes to clutter and household confusion.

## One small change

When you've got a clearer picture of your partner's good and bad points, don't jump in with both feet. Instead, ask them to sort out one specific area that's driving you nuts. Be prepared to trade – ask them in return if there's a cluttered zone that they'd like you to deal with.

## Update

Next week talk again calmly and see how you've both progressed. Each agree to drop one more bad habit – like damp towels on the floor or DVDs out of their covers.

'Marriage is not just spiritual communion – it is also remembering to take the trash out.' Dr Joyce Brothers, family psychologist

ENCOURAGE OTHERS IN YOUR HOUSEHOLD

## *Activity*
# Your partner's hoarding habits

If you're getting increasingly bothered by your partner's messy ways, before you blow up, consider:

- Have they always been this way? Were they a keen collector before you lived together?

- Did you think that moving in together would change their behaviour?

- What drives you crazy – pants on the floor or newspapers everywhere?

- What do they like to hoard? It could be anything from shoes to hundreds of carrier bags.

- How have you handled this in the past? Have you nagged or thrown away contentious objects leading to major rows?

- Are fights about clutter masking other touchy issues like money troubles, working hours and too many hours slumped in front of the TV?

- Do you each have your own space where you can let your hair down and be creative?

- Is your partner more organised than you in certain ways? Do they have positive habits that you'd like to copy?

- Do you credit them with any improvements they've made over the years?

ENCOURAGE OTHERS IN YOUR HOUSEHOLD

Children are inundated with possessions in our consumer society, and jumbled bedrooms are the inevitable outcome. Many houses feel more like toy shops than relaxing family homes.

## *Activity*

# Climb the kids' clutter mountain

There's no one formula that will work throughout childhood to conquer clutter. Break tasks down into age-appropriate chunks like sorting out one toy box at a time. Go through school books one weekend and their wardrobe the next. It's not going to get straightened overnight so be patient!

### Babies and toddlers

- For a new baby compile a gift or christening list so you get what you need.

- Create a memory box for your baby. Resist the temptation to preserve every toy and piece of clothing.

- My friend has just had a new baby daughter, she's not likely to want dozens of pretty pink dresses. So I'm going to give her something useful but cute like pyjamas.

- Swap with friends or borrow or buy second-hand baby equipment.

- Join a toy library so your kids can enjoy new toys without adding to the clutter.

'It is not giving children more that spoils them; it is giving them more to avoid confrontation.' John Gray, relationship expert and author

ENCOURAGE OTHERS IN YOUR HOUSEHOLD

114

## Primary school children

- Kids love to make a mess, but from an early age, they need to learn that tidying up is part of playing. Nurseries and schools have clearly-marked containers so toys can be put away easily.

- Always make sure that storage is at the right height for young children and is labelled with simple words or pictures.

- Be patient – if your seven-year-old has never decluttered his room, he may not be keen to start.

- Get kids used to passing on outgrown toys and books. A sale at their school may fire their enthusiasm.

- Don't expect them to be tidier than you. If your bedroom is a tip, they'll see that as normal.

- Use a storage box to conserve special school projects.

## Teenagers

- Teenagers are under incredible pressure from their peers and society to look good, to have designer trainers and to carry the latest must-have mobile phone. None of this comes cheap and can cause family friction as they strive to keep up with the latest trends.

- Teenagers love to create a nest in their rooms. It's a time of change and creativity and goes hand in hand with clutter. Set down some basic bedroom ground rules like no mouldy food and that only clothes in the linen basket get washed. Agree that their make-up and dirty socks stay out of the living room.

ENCOURAGE OTHERS IN YOUR HOUSEHOLD

Do you sometimes feel you're losing the battle against a tide of plastic toys and a burgeoning collection of computer games? The relentless targeting of even very young children by TV adverts means that their consumer cravings are constantly stimulated.

## Shocking facts

◆ In the UK parents spend £400 million a year on party bags alone. The average cost is £10 but many are worth as much as £20.
◆ Middle–class kids have an average of 70 new toys a year.
◆ Eight in ten UK kids have their own TV set.
◆ Children see a staggering 10 000 TV adverts every year. No wonder they're so clued up about what they want!

### TOP TIP

◆ Resist buying every new toy or gizmo as soon as it hits the market. Most will wind up as one-minute wonders. Rent DVDs or games instead.
◆ Avoid competing with other parents. Although this is easier said than done, if your neighbour spends hundreds on a fabulous horse-riding party, you don't have to outdo them.
◆ Don't feel like a skinflint if you say no to expensive purchases that you can't afford.

ENCOURAGE OTHERS IN YOUR HOUSEHOLD

*Activity*

## Reduce kids' clutter in the long term

Of course you want the best for your kids, but it's important to question whether they need so much stuff to have a fulfilling life. Just like adults, kids can get overloaded by too many possessions.

**Change habits**

- Curb compulsive gift buying. How often do you give presents to your kids outside celebrations? Has it become routine to buy them a DVD or a new toy every weekend? Over time, the kids will come to expect this as their right, not as a special treat!

- Ask grandparents and other relatives not to shower your kids with presents every time they visit.

- Give older children a set amount of pocket money or a clothing allowance and be specific about what it covers. Then resist pester power when the money runs out.

- Start pocket money young so your children are aware of the cost of toys, sweets and comics.

- Set a budget at Christmas and birthdays. They may want a £300 set of drums but if you can't afford it, don't creep into debt. Also, limit the number of presents you give at one time. Bulk-giving is overwhelming and devalues the experience.

ENCOURAGE OTHERS IN YOUR HOUSEHOLD

Our beloved pets don't have their own credit cards yet somehow they acquire loads of toys, towels, blankets, grooming equipment, food bowls, medicines, leads and pet carriers.

We all love to spoil our animals with treats but are we overdoing it? Is your dog better dressed than you with a diamanté collar and designer coat for every day of the week?

## *Activity*

# Sort through your pet's possessions

Your cat doesn't need five food bowls or a basket full of toys so get decluttering!

- Set up a folder for each of your pets with important information, including vaccination records, kennel numbers and insurance documents. Put your pet's name and the vet's phone number on the outside.

- Enter key numbers for your pet into your mobile, address book or personal organiser.

- I like to give my dog Barney consumable gifts such as bits of apple or a chew.

- Have your mobile number on your pet's collar and make sure they're micro chipped.

- Check whether local animal charities would appreciate your pet's surplus possessions.

- Don't save unused equipment – if you've not had a rabbit since your child was little, why hang on to the hutch?

- Never leave pet toys on the floor. Once playtime is over, put them away until next time.

## *Activity*
## Check your progress

How's your living room looking today? If there was a knock on the door would you feel comfortable inviting a guest in for a cup of tea? If not, spring into action and single-mindedly curb the clutter.

'No animal should ever jump up on the dining-room furniture unless absolutely sure that he can hold his own in the conversation.'
Fran Lebowitz, US writer and humourist

ENCOURAGE OTHERS IN YOUR HOUSEHOLD

Whether you share with flatmates or teenagers, it's important to agree on basic standards and routines to keep your home in order.

## CASE STUDY

No-one in the Miller family had seen their bedroom carpets for years. The two children, Millie aged six and Ben aged nine, followed their parents' example and were fast turning into hoarders who kept every toy and game they'd ever owned. The problem was they were learning little respect for their possessions, which lay around getting broken and mislaid. Their generous parents would treat them to something new every week and shower them with gifts on special occasions.

Both parents worked full-time and found that keeping order in the house slipped down the priority list. When the kids finally swung into action and filled a bag for Oxfam, their mum panicked. She started taking things out because she was horrified that they were throwing away things that had cost a lot of money. She eventually realised that she was modelling hoarding behaviour and needed to encourage them to give away toys they didn't play with any more.

Because time was so tight in the week, it was agreed the kids would spend half an hour tidying up their rooms every Saturday before ballet and theatre classes. Once a month everyone would fill a bag to take to charity. Even though the kids kicked off at first, they're enjoying their bedrooms so much more now!

## Beware resistance

Change unsettles other people and they may find subtle or not-so-subtle ways of undermining your resolve. If you've had organising splurges in the past, they may hope you'll lose interest soon. Your steadiness will be an example to everyone you live with – that you're determined this time. But don't become a martyr and constantly clear up after other people!

*Activity*

## Work together to create routines

- Make a decluttering day part of your annual household calendar.

- Schedule a clearout and then get the whole household to spend a day selling the clutter at a car boot sale. End the ritual with a reward like a barbecue or a trip to the theatre.

- Create a culture of donating to charity and always have a bag on the go that everyone can add to. If you haven't got a car, use one of the bona fide charity collection bags that come through the front door.

- Have realistic expectations about your home. It will reflect the ebb and flow of life. Surface clutter will accumulate from time to time so set aside a slot at the weekend for everyone to pitch in.

- Allow others some slack in personal areas like bedrooms but expect everyone to remove clutter from communal areas.

- Rotate dull tasks so no-one feels hard done by or gets bored.

'Housework is something you do that nobody notices until you don't do it.' Anonymous

ENCOURAGE OTHERS IN YOUR HOUSEHOLD

# Your notes

CHAPTER 10

# SORT OUT SENTIMENTAL BELONGINGS

It's part of human nature to attach meaning and memories to our possessions. As babies we clung to our comfort blankets and the beloved bear that went with us everywhere. As adults too, we like to surround ourselves with cherished objects that confirm our identity and our place in the universe. The problem really kicks in when this sentimentality takes over and you find it heartbreaking to let go of your toddler's scribbles or birthday cards from ten years ago. Even a pine cone can feel invaluable because it reminds you of an autumn walk in the woods.

## Activity

## Sentimental hoarder quiz

You don't have to be cold and unemotional or chuck out items that have a special meaning for you. It's important to celebrate and cherish significant belongings. But what you do have to guard against is the automatic reaction to hold on to things from your past, simply because they were given to you or were once important.

Score 1 for every 'yes':

- Do you find it impossible to reject any photo even if it's out of focus?

- Do you hoard all your birthday cards from years ago?

- Are you loathe to discard any of your children's artwork or baby clothes?

- Do you collect souvenirs from every trip or holiday?

- Do you preserve every love letter you've ever received?

- Do you believe that once you're given a present you should have it forever?

SORT OUT SENTIMENTAL BELONGINGS

- Do you cling to clothes because you remember the times you wore them?

- Does every decluttering decision feel exhausting because it brings up lot of memories?

- Do you have boxes of toys from your own childhood?

- Do you collect programmes and ticket stubs to remind you of great evenings out?

- Have you inherited possessions you don't need but feel obliged to keep?

- Are you worried that if you let things go you'll lose a core part of yourself?

**Your score**

1–3: Your sentimental tendencies are under control.

4–7: You're beginning to lose your way – time to be more selective.

8–12: You truly are a nostalgic hoarder – your goal is to loosen the past's grip on you.

## A mini step

Even if you're soft-hearted, make today the day you declutter one thing, even if it's just a Christmas or birthday card.

## Letting go

Over the coming days you're going to tackle the sentimental clutter that's weighing you down. It may be a vulnerable period as you come face to face with emotional memories. But it will help you move on. You'll feel lighter and freer as you live more in the present and less in the past.

SORT OUT SENTIMENTAL BELONGINGS

Precious memories deserve to be cherished and kept in a beautiful container. Your memory box is the place for storing the first baby shoes, the hand-drawn card, the key to your first flat and other similarly evocative memories.

# Activity
## Create a memory box

- For your memory box you could choose a trunk or a leather box. Search around your home and see if you've anything suitable. If not visit the shops today or look online and choose a box that really lifts your heart.

- Your kids also need a memory box – choose significant early-childhood items they will enjoy looking back at when they're adults. As they get older encourage them to add special birthday cards or beloved toys they've outgrown.

- Your memory box is not a static affair – over the years you'll continue to add treasures.

- As time passes, let go of some memories that aren't happy. If you loathe your ex-partner, you may prefer to burn their letters rather than keep them in the memory box!

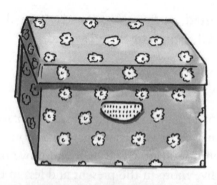

## TOP TIP

◆ Remember, you're collecting together special memories –
you want the edited highlights, not a home totally
dedicated to the past. Looking in the memory box will
remind you of good times in your life.

'We spend most of our time in a kind of horizontal thinking. We
move along the surface of things ... but there are times when we
stop. We sit still. We lose ourselves in a pile of leaves or its
memory. We listen and breezes from a whole other world begin to
whisper.' James Carroll, international expert on future trends

In the run-up to Christmas, shoppers often have a glazed, slightly desperate look in their eyes, which isn't surprising when you consider how tricky buying presents can be, even for those closest to us. Despite our best intentions and care, some presents will inevitably fall wide of the mark. Receiving unwanted gifts can also be a minefield leading to guilt, clutter and even resentment.

## *Activity*
# Restore pleasure to gifts

Grab a notebook and write down:

- presents you received last Christmas

- presents you were given for your last birthday.

Chances are you can only remember the real winners and the stinkers you were given!

It's also unlikely that you'll remember many of the presents you bought last Christmas. Test yourself by trying to recall what you gave everyone in your family.

It's not easy, is it? The upside of this is that, before long, most people forget what they've given you as well. Bear this in mind when you make decluttering decisions about gifts – it's not as all-important as you thought.

## TOP TIP

A genuine gift is chosen with love and given freely. Accept it graciously in the spirit in which it was chosen. After that it's yours to do with as you please. If it's not your taste, then give it to charity.

## Dealing with unwanted gifts

Think about the stinkers – the Santa earrings, the overpowering pot pourri, the dull comedy book and ask yourself:

◆ Why are you holding on to them?
◆ Does shoving them in the cupboard make you feel better?
◆ Do you imagine the giver would want you to hold on to something you don't like?

## *Activity* Let them go!

Unearth five unwanted presents now and take them straight to the charity shop. Don't let yourself be overcome by indecision. Remember, you have the right to a clutter-free home and to do what you want with your possessions.

## Giving presents

◆ Choose one great gift rather than lots of little trinkets.
◆ Never ask about your gift later. You'll be putting the recipient in an awkward position if they didn't like it.
◆ For people who have everything, choose a consumable present like a good bottle of wine, an exotic bunch of flowers or a pampering gift like a reflexology voucher or a spa day.
◆ Surprises can be wonderful but are a high-risk strategy. Instead ask people what they'd like!
◆ Set a cash limit for adults at Christmas. The gifts can be inventive and fun, and definitely kinder to your credit card bill.
◆ Celebrations bring a new onslaught of possessions to your home. To maintain balance, make sure you have a declutter around your birthday and New Year.

SORT OUT SENTIMENTAL BELONGINGS

If your parents were hoarders they probably stashed away boxes of your childhood toys, books and school projects. Did you carry these off to your adult home and promptly stick them in the loft? Do you feel part of your identity would vanish without four Sindy dolls or six albums of football cards?

*Activity*

## Be sentimental but selective

### Toys

Assemble all your childhood memorabilia. As you look at each item, tune in to your memories. If something has positive associations and significance do you want to hold on to it? Or would you rather let someone else take pleasure in it? Perhaps your nephew would make good use of the Scalextric rather than it lying neglected in the garage.

### Games

Do you still have sets of Cluedo and Monopoly? Why not dust these off and enjoy playing them with friends and your kids. But if they bring back memories of miserable family fights on Sunday afternoons, don't hesitate to give them away.

### School books

Do you really treasure every Geography notebook or spelling book from your school days? Preserve a couple that make you smile and recycle the rest.

### Children's story books

Classics like Heidi and Roald Dahl stories are difficult to part with. Again, keep your favourites and pass on the others to charity or to children you know.

SORT OUT SENTIMENTAL BELONGINGS

## Collectors' items

If your James Bond Aston Martin is boxed in mint condition it will be worth a few quid. Are you keeping similar collectables for your pension? Fair enough, but do think twice about buying toys as investments or hoarding your kids' cast-offs.

What's more important to you – a clutter-free home or endless boxes full of Beanie babies or Dinky toys?

## Possessions left at your parents' home

If you left home years ago but still expect your parents to store your train set, your teenage wardrobe and much more, think again. Once you have your own home it really is your responsibility to collect what's yours and sort it out. Don't think of it as a chore – you're bound to have a laugh when you come across some of the bizarre stuff you used to treasure!

Even though digital cameras have taken over, most people have drawers and boxes full of old prints. If you love recording holidays, celebrations and your family's antics this may prove to be a marathon task. I know sorting out photos can be scary but do make a start today. You may choose to complete this on a winter weekend or in the long summer evenings.

## Your camera equipment

How many of your cameras have you used recently? Disposable cameras and films have use-by dates so check whether they're still viable. Finish off half-shot films that have been lurking in cameras for a while. Then give away or sell any excess camera equipment.

*Activity*

## Get pleasure from your photos

Concentrate today on the packets of prints.

**Get rid of the clutter**

- Get a box and collect up all photos and albums. You may need more than one box if you're a keen photographer.

- Begin going through your photos, discarding any that are out of focus and any obscure scenic spots.

- Question the belief that every photo is sacred. Instead, think like a professional photographer – you're aiming for a few great shots.

SORT OUT SENTIMENTAL BELONGINGS

- Twenty photos of the conservatory being built are hardly necessary. One is enough!

- If you've dozens of similar photos of your son's first birthday or friend's wedding, insert some into Christmas or birthday cards. Or add photos of friends in 80s fashions to make them smile.

- Inherited family photos are tricky – especially if you haven't a clue who half the people are. Is there a relative researching your family tree who could help you out? If not, stick them in a box in the loft for future generations to pore over. In the meantime make an album of ancestors you can identify.

- Store negatives properly. It's best to use a professional ring binder box.

**Display your newly pared-down collection**

- Celebrate good memories by putting photos on the fridge, making collages or sending them to people straight away.

- Frequently change the photos in frames to keep things feeling fresh. If you have dozens of baby photos scattered around, do you ever look at them? Try packing half away for a few months and see if you miss them.

- Do write on the back of photos who they are and where they were taken. You might not remember in 20 years!

- Enjoy arranging your favourites into gorgeous albums.

SORT OUT SENTIMENTAL BELONGINGS

From early childhood, collecting is highly enjoyable. Children have fads and phases along with their friends. One minute it's the latest action figures, then it's fossils or football cards. Later, in teenage years, it's all boy-band posters or computer games.

Our enthusiasms and interests also ebb and flow as adults. Yet hoarders hold on to teddy-bear collections or model soldiers long after losing interest. Collecting can cause friction with others – either because of all the time involved or the sheer amount of space the objects take up.

## CASE STUDY

James thought of himself as a collector rather than a hoarder. He couldn't resist the lure of machines that needed fixing up. He had given little thought to how all the computers, portable TVs and period gramophones were cluttering up his house. He was convinced he was sitting on a small fortune. His partner saw it differently as she fought her way through the mayhem in her living room. They reached a compromise – James treated himself to a large shed-workshop and agreed his collections stayed out of their home.

## Family patterns

Are your parents and siblings also avid collectors? If your family places a high value on collecting it will feel uncomfortable to alter your habits. Don't involve them in your decision-making as they'll expect you to keep everything.

*Activity*

## Recognise the fine line between collecting and hoarding

First make a list of all your different collections. For each one, ask yourself:

- How much pleasure do you get from using or looking at it?
- How often do you add to your collection?
- Is it beginning to overrun your home?
- Are you spending more than you can afford on expensive additions like rare LPs or antique clocks?
- Does your collection feel more like a compulsion than a choice?

## TOP TIP

Tackle each collection in turn with an open-minded attitude.

- ◆ You don't have to 'complete' your collection. If you don't like part of your collection, then sell it or give it away without guilt.
- ◆ If you decide to forgo all your silver teapots do check out eBay or speak to your local auction or antique shop about resale value.
- ◆ If you keep memorabilia for investment purposes, are you prepared to store it for many years?
- ◆ Stop and reconsider before launching into new crazes. Just because you've got a couple of fridge magnets, fight the impulse to buy one from every place you visit!
- ◆ Don't become over-sentimental about all the hours you spent scouring boot fairs and collectors' markets. You had fun at the time, but it doesn't mean you have to keep your finds forever.

SORT OUT SENTIMENTAL BELONGINGS

Losing someone dear to you is a devastating experience and can take many years to come to terms with. Part of the grieving process is wanting to hold on to memories and surrounding ourselves with tangible reminders of their presence.

*Activity*

## Keep cherished possessions

After a loss, trust yourself to know when you feel ready to go through your loved one's things.

- If financial constraints mean you're under pressure to clear and sell a relative's flat or move on from the home you shared with your partner or spouse, consider renting a temporary self-storage unit. This will give you healing space before making difficult decisions.

- As time moves on, you may not want to keep everything you inherited. It's normal to feel ambivalent and disloyal saying goodbye to things that belonged to someone you loved. Set guilt aside. You're not dishonouring your love for them.

- Celebrate their memory by keeping treasures that recall happy memories.

- Take a photo of anything you're letting go but would like a permanent reminder of.

- Sell things you don't need and put the money towards something that will bring you pleasure or take a much-needed holiday.

SORT OUT SENTIMENTAL BELONGINGS

- If your loved one wasn't specific about their wishes, imagine what they would have liked to happen to their possessions. If they cared deeply about world issues, then give their clothes and books to Oxfam. Ask friends and family if there's a memento they would like.

- Let go of unhappy memories associated with illness such as hospital notes and medical equipment.

- Make a memory box for special things like a beloved jumper, book or their favourite watch.

- If many years have passed and you can't bring yourself to part with anything, do speak to a bereavement counsellor.

- Sorting out their possessions is part of the tough process of letting go and acceptance. Always be compassionate and tender with yourself. Accept your emotional vulnerability and have someone close by you can call on for support.

## Clarify your own wishes

Many people don't like to contemplate making a will or what will happen to their worldly goods when they are gone. But if you care deeply about who inherits your prized possessions, it's important to get this down in a legal document.

SORT OUT SENTIMENTAL BELONGINGS

Memories are a vital part of who we are. Yet if we kept everything with an associated memory, we'd never be able to get through the front door. People can become deeply attached to things and wax lyrical about pieces of wood, shoelaces from a favourite pair of shoes or even the chip pan!

'We must never allow the future to be weighed down by memory. For children have no past, and that is the whole secret of the magical innocence of their smiles.' Milan Kundera, author

*Activity*

# Don't be a slave to sentiment

To keep your life in order you're going to have to change the way you value nostalgic items. A Christmas card could be of great value because it's a collage by your grandchild or it might be a mundane one from your optician. The first one deserves pride of place on your mantelpiece or in your memory box; the latter belongs in the recycling.

If you've been clinging on to unhappy memories such as application forms for jobs you didn't get or love letters that make you miserable, let them go today.

**In future**

- Abandon all-or-nothing thinking such as 'I must save all postcards or all of my kids' artwork.'

- Use the 'smile test' (see Day 92) to help you to decide. If the mere sight of something makes you break into a grin, then that's a keeper. These happy memories are the ones you want to cherish.

- Trust your heart. It's always up to you what you choose to keep. If your partner is a hoarder, don't let them pressure you.

- The world won't end if you let go of remnants of your past. Instead, feel as though you're lightening your life and opening up the future.

SORT OUT SENTIMENTAL BELONGINGS

# Your notes

# LIMIT LEISURE
# EQUIPMENT

Imaginative people see infinite ways to transform mundane objects into something beautiful. The downside to this vision and talent is it's much harder to part with scraps of material, buttons or wrapping paper. The artist Francis Bacon said of his cluttered studio, ' I feel at home here in this chaos because chaos suggests images to me.' He hoarded newspapers, photos, catalogues — anything that would inspire him.

Unlike Francis Bacon, very few of us have our own studio, so if your spare room, living room and bedroom are swamped with art supplies, take stock today.

## *Activity*

## Streamline art and craft materials

Designate a specific area where you can create your works of art, even if it's only a corner of the spare room. Don't let your artistic projects wander throughout your home.

- How many half-finished projects do you have on the go? If a needlepoint cushion has been untouched for the past four years, are you really going to take it up again? If not, pass it on to a friend or charity shop.

- Don't feel you have to archive unsuccessful sketches or artwork.

- Good storage is key when it comes to organising your craft equipment. You want to spend time being creative not looking for a lost stencil. Store like with like so all glitter pots are together and all crochet hooks.

- Transparent boxes make the best storage (buy at stationers or good DIY shops). Cutlery trays inside drawers are useful for small tools.

- If you've a lifetime's supply of paper, pencils and craft materials, resist the temptation to make weekly visits to the art and craft shop.

- Follow the one in, one out policy to stop your home bulging at the seams. For every new thing you buy, let something similar go.

- Think carefully before giving your works of art to friends and family. How are you going to feel if they don't showcase them? If you do give them, do so freely and accept the other person's right to do with them as they please.

- If your kids are producing daily drawings and models from nursery school, display them while they're new and then only keep the cream in their memory box.

- Host a swapping session for other craft fans where you exchange excess materials for something you'd actually use. It's free and it's fun.

## Enjoy your personal style

Most importantly of all, know yourself. Do you work well surrounded by visual images like Francis Bacon or do you need a little more clear space for your creativity?

LIMIT LEISURE EQUIPMENT

Is your house littered with niggling DIY tasks that need attention, like a dripping tap or a curtain pole that's coming adrift? Dissatisfaction will begin to build up because incomplete jobs are a kind of clutter. They'll make your home feel neglected and unloved.

## *Activity*

## Deal with unfinished DIY

The first half of today's challenge is to list any outstanding DIY. Note any equipment you need to buy, who's going to do the job, whether it is urgent or non-urgent, and a date by which it will be achieved.

| Task | Parts needed | Who | When |
|------|-------------|-----|------|
| Dripping kitchen tap | Washer | Myself | Saturday |
| Replace cracked bedroom window | – | Glazier | Urgent ring today |

Be practical – you can't catch up with a big backlog in one day so prioritise the urgent areas and work your way through your list.

### DIY tools

Focus DIY found that two-thirds of men take pride in their toolboxes and believe that it's their duty to be good at DIY. Apparently, 88 per cent of men would be pleased to receive a tool for a special gift, compared to 11 per cent of women.

This is an amazing statistic when you realise that the average electric drill only gets 15 minutes use in its entire lifetime. There must be a lot of unused equipment in those toolboxes!

LIMIT LEISURE EQUIPMENT

**Declutter your tools**

- Organise your tools so they're accessible next time a DIY-crisis arises.

- Buy decent tool boxes and containers for all your screws and nails.

- Only hang on to the most effective screwdrivers and hammers.

- Hire tools rather than buying them if it's a one-off job like wallpaper stripping.

- Recycle broken metal tools.

## TOP TIP

- Dismiss the idea that you can never have too many tools. You want an efficient set, not a collection!
- Don't borrow tools from friends and neighbours and then hold on to them for months. Make a point of returning them promptly with a gift to show your appreciation. A survey found that a third of people in the UK won't lend their tools – probably because they've had bad experiences in the past.
- Question your knee-jerk response to hoarding components from obsolete appliances and countless pairs of old trousers for any DIY crisis.
- Don't buy the washer for the tap and then consider the job done. You actually need to fit it!

'One only needs two tools in life: WD-40 to make things go, and duct tape to make them stop.' G.M. Weilacher

LIMIT LEISURE EQUIPMENT

We're constantly being told to get moving and stop being couch potatoes. Yet there's little evidence that this advice is driving people's behaviour. The rowing machines bought in January are used a handful of times and then shoved into the garage in February. Even if you're a keen athlete and live, breathe and dream of sports, evidence of past fitness enthusiasms may be spread throughout your home.

## *Activity*

## Reduce your exercise equipment

Don't let neglected exercise clutter take up valuable space. You should already have made headway with sports clothing, aerobics videos and exercise kit kept under the bed. Today tackle any remaining sporting equipment that needs decluttering and organising.

- Incorporate exercise into your routine. Buy a pedometer and see if you can achieve the recommended 10,000 daily steps.

- Choose exercise you enjoy, perhaps with a sociable element, like five-a-side football or badminton.

- Sell equipment you'll never use again rather than sticking it in the garage.

- Know yourself and your lifestyle. Set attainable goals like swimming once a week. That way you'll achieve your target and enjoy yourself.

- Put a time limit on how long you keep paraphernalia you've stopped using. My yoga mat's gathering dust and if I don't use it in the next couple of months, it's off to the charity shop!

LIMIT LEISURE EQUIPMENT

## TOP TIP

◆ You won't get fit spending your leisure time watching football or playing motor racing games on the PC!

◆ Don't con yourself that buying expensive machines will miraculously transform your behaviour. If you're truly committed to a home gym, then look for second-hand equipment in good condition.

◆ Avoid nagging your kids to turn off the computer or TV. Instead incorporate exercise as a fun activity like a kick around in the park, ice-skating or rollerblading.

'One step at a time is good walking.' Chinese proverb

LIMIT LEISURE EQUIPMENT

# Your notes

# CHAPTER 12

## PURGE YOUR PAPERWORK

## DAY 64: PAPER CLUTTER

Paper, paper everywhere … But can you lay your hand on the gas bill or your dog's vaccination card when you need it? If paper has become your nemesis, and the disorder is growing daily, get a grip now.

*Activity*

## Assess your personal paperwork crisis

**Paper chase quiz**

Score 1 point for each 'yes'.

Set a timer for ten minutes and find the following things. Make sure you only score 1 for each item when you actually lay your hands on it!

- House insurance policy
- Birthday card, envelope and stamp
- Latest bank statement
- Last electricity bill
- Instruction manual for current mobile phone
- Dentist's phone number
- Stapler
- TV licence
- Passport
- Your address book

**Your score**

Less than 2: Your paperwork is chaotic!
3–6: You've got some systems, but need to upgrade.
7–10: Well done – you're really on top of paper!

## Be realistic

Sorting your paperwork is the most time-consuming part of getting organised. Either set aside a quiet weekend for a paper purge or commit 30 minutes a day until things are back on track.

It's best to have an overview of the whole topic before launching in. Spend a few minutes today reading through the rest of this chapter.

*Activity*

## Take two small steps

- Ditch blotchy biros and fading felt tips. Keep a container for pens by the phone (an old mug will do for this) and another by the front door and on your desk. Pens seem to have their own lifeforce and drift from place to place so rehome them daily.

- Get a box or plastic crate and for ten minutes collect up scattered paperwork. Having it all together will speed things up when the sorting and filing begins in a couple of days.

'Have confidence if you have done a little thing well, you can do a bigger thing well too.' David Storey

A common mistake is to randomly buy folders, filing boxes and storage products to fight back paper chaos. These often lie around unused, exacerbating the problem and adding to the clutter.

## *Activity*
## Stock take your stationery

You need basic stationery supplies to manage your paperwork. Your first task is to organise all the stationery you've already got.

### Set up a stock area

- Collect together all empty folders. Use a box to house them temporarily.

- Allocate a shelf for your envelopes, paper and labels.

- Stationery like staplers, rubbers and correcting fluid can be stored in a basket on your desk. Or use a drawer divider to separate out pens from post-it notes.

- You may want to duplicate supplies in different parts of the house. Keep a stash of stamps in the kitchen drawer as well as in your office. But don't scatter them everywhere!

- A pretty tin can hold your birthday cards and note cards. Keep this well stocked – we all need thank-you cards at short notice.

### Review your stock checklist

Now you've got a precise picture of what you already own, check you have a basic starter kit:

- One individual 'action' tray. This is for papers that need attention such as unpaid bills or letters that need replies.

- 20 transparent document folders and labels.

PURGE YOUR PAPERWORK

- Stapler and staples, hole punch, paper clips, permanent marker and highlighter pens and post-it notes.

- Six box files – get these in different colours so you can identify the contents at a glance. These are ideal for bulky stuff like car manuals.

- Two ringbinder files – good for recipes and leisure articles.

- Bulldog clips or one clipboard – for holding unpaid bills or outstanding paperwork.

- If you have a filing cabinet, make sure you have hanging files and clip-on labels.

- Shredder – buy the best one you can afford as the cheap ones can be ineffective.

There's more background on how to use the stationery later in this chapter.

**Buy basic stationery**

Now shop for any of the above kit that's missing. The quantities given are just for starters. It's always better to go back and top up than finish up with piles of unnecessary folders.

## TOP TIP

- There are fantastic savings on stationery if you buy in bulk. This works if you've got enough storage. But restricted storage will lead to boxes of printer paper and notepads cluttering the floor area.

- Delay buying big items like filing cabinets until you have a better idea of what size you need. As you streamline your paperwork, this will become a lot clearer.

PURGE YOUR PAPERWORK

Even the word filing seems to strike dread into people's hearts! Paper pilers believe that filing a document is equivalent to flinging it on the fire. It will never see daylight again. So they construct piles on their desks, in the kitchen, on the floor and trust an invoice will reappear when needed. Perhaps it will eventually, but think of all those lost hours spent scrabbling for misplaced documents.

## *Activity*

## Set up a filing system for important paperwork

Essential information like insurance policies, maintenance contracts and mortgage statements are fundamental tools for an orderly life. Your aim is to create an effective system that will give you instant access to any document.

If filing has fazed you in the past, be brave and make a start today.

**Filing**

- Choose simple filing categories. These could include health, school, car, life insurance, pets, etc. Avoid folders called 'miscellaneous' or 'household'. Be specific – use 'gas bills' or 'Primrose playgroup'.

- Next, label a transparent folder with each subject heading. I lay these out on the floor and then get sorting. Leave decluttering at this stage – just stick all the home phone bills into one labelled folder and the mobile bills into another and keep going.

- Having all your equipment manuals in one place will ensure quick retrieval next time you can't fathom out a feature on your DVD player.

PURGE YOUR PAPERWORK

- Put current paperwork like unpaid bills into your action tray. Make a note on your to-do list and highlight urgent tasks.

**Streamlining**

- The fine-tuning of each folder is the next step. It's a major project that can be worked on over the medium term. Tackle each individually – one day you declutter the car file, the next it's the health file.

- File documents in date order with the newest at the front of each folder as these are the ones you're most likely to use.

- Be confident about making decisions. You know you don't need your cat's pet insurance from four years ago. Work the one in, one out policy and chuck last year's when this year's is filed.

- If certain folders are still bulky even when you've pared them down, then subdivide them.

- When you've finished sorting the folders, it's easier to see if you need a filing cabinet or can get by with a handful of box files.

# Paper perils

- Avoid creating an overcomplicated system. You don't need separate folders for car tax and car insurance. Put them all in the same file.
- Stop hoarding pointless paper. Ask yourself what's the worst that could happen if you didn't have your student rent book!
- Filing is an action not a pile. Always take the extra step and file the instant you've finished dealing with a document.
- Sentimental letters belong in your memory box not your filing cabinet.

Money oils all our lives. Yet the relationship between how much money we have and how much we spend has become distorted. If we want something, many of us don't save up or even check our bank balance. Instead we grab our credit card and secure what our heart's desire. The problem is that as debts and confusion increase it's common to adopt a head-in-the-sand approach. We stop opening our post, we never check our statements and the stress builds and builds.

## *Activity*

## Fine-tune your financial filing

Unpaid bills and penalties for forgotten parking fines will soon be a thing of the past.

Create clearly labelled folders for each financial category:

- bills – electricity, gas, phone, council tax, insurance policies, mortgage or rent

- savings and investments

- tax records

- bank accounts

- credit and store cards.

## Shred

With the rise in identity theft it's crucial to shred financial documents and utility bills, which can be used to apply for fraudulent credit. Buy a heavy-duty shredder and then recycle the shredded paper.

## Debt

Talk to someone from an advice agency like the Citizens' Advice Bureau if debts are out of hand. You'll need to discuss the real state of affairs, so gather all your financial documents in one place. It may help to have a non-judgemental friend around to support you when you finally open bills, letters from your bank and final demands.

### *Activity* Good habits

Don't be afraid of your finances. Use simple methods to make everything run smoothly.

- Check receipts off against your bank and credit card statements. Tell your bank or credit card company immediately if any unusual activity has taken place.

- Simplify your life by reducing the number of cards that you use. Store cards are an expensive way of getting credit. Be bold and cut up excess cards today.

- Check with the tax office or your accountant how long to retain financial information for. Some records, like income tax, need to be kept safe for years. Others, like utility bills, are generally only for your own reference. Store a year's worth of gas bills and shred the oldest one when filing the new bill.

- Pay bills wherever possible by direct debit. Use a clipboard for any other bills that need to be paid. Find a regular time each month to sort these out.

- Use online banking if you find it convenient to sort your finances during the evening or weekend.

- Banks and building societies will provide folders to keep all your statements together.

PURGE YOUR PAPERWORK

Most of the envelopes that drop through the letterbox six days a week are junk mail. The growth of email has done little to stem the relentless flow of marketing material. But among the dross are important letters that need to be dealt with. Ignored, the growing piles of mystery envelopes become more intimidating with each passing day and life can quickly spiral out of control.

## *Activity*

## Redefine your attitude to the post

First blitz the mound of unopened post. Every letter you receive requires a mini-decision from you. Use the following criteria to help you make rapid, stress-free choices.

| The letter | Example | Action |
|---|---|---|
| Pure junk | Useless sales circular | Remove personal details and recycle |
| Relevant document but needs no further action | TV license | File at once |
| Important and needs action | Bills to pay, letter to reply to | Either do it straight away if it takes less than a minute <br> *or* <br> Add to action tray and make a note on your to-do list |
| Potentially interesting | Holiday brochure | If in doubt, chuck it out <br> *or* <br> Add to reading pile with today's date <br> Declutter this pile regularly |

**Do**

● Open all post. It's tempting to discard junk mail but it's not always possible to judge letters by their envelope. The odd dull-looking one could contain a cheque for a share dividend or an important message from your bank.

● Remove and shred all personal details before recycling.

● Create a designated area with your shredder, recycling and filing. Deal with your post here every day.

● Ask to be removed from mailing lists for products you're not interested in any more Register your name with The Mail Preference Service to stop getting unsolicited post. Go to: www.mpsonline.org.uk

## TOP TIP

◆ Don't overvalue unimportant circulars. Your priority is to stay on top of essential documents and keep your life in order.

◆ No more procrastination! It's straightforward to deal with a few letters but if they build up, the backlog will become daunting.

◆ Put letters for posting on the hall table as a visual reminder. If you stick them in your bag, they may lurk forgotten for days.

PURGE YOUR PAPERWORK

So far we've looked at how to manage important documents and financial records. But for many people, that's not the crux of their paper problem. They love to collect and hoard newspapers, magazines, brochures, interesting features and special offers.

## CASE STUDY

Lucy, a true paper hoarder, loved leaflets and brochures – in fact, anything that contained facts. Every day she printed screeds of offers and interesting features off the web. She told me if her flat was big enough she'd never part with any of this. For her, information was precious currency and it had to be kept. She found it difficult to distinguish between the significance of her bank statements and a leaflet for a Pilates class.

Her worst fear was throwing away something she'd later need. But the irony was that the more she kept, the more chaotic her flat became. She couldn't lay her hands on documents when she needed them anyway! Painful as it was for her, she began to acknowledge that not all paper is equal, and out-of-date details are useless. She was always going to be attracted to ripping out newspaper articles and picking up leaflets. But creating folders and decluttering them every year meant that she didn't feel deprived – but still kept her life in basic order.

## TOP TIP

◆ Accept that the more paper you hoard, the more time you're going to have to spend filing and organising it. We live in an era of information overload and unless you're discriminating, your home will soon be engulfed in paper.

PURGE YOUR PAPERWORK

*Activity*

## Re-evaluate your relationship with low-priority information

Choose energising music and get ready for a ruthless paper purge!

- On Day 32 we looked at how to regain control of magazines, catalogues and newspapers in your living room. But if you have stashes elsewhere in your home, tackle them now. Before creating permanent collections of gardening or craft magazines, mull over whether you're likely to refer to them again.

- Ideas for weekend breaks or interior design can be useful. But don't pull out every wine column from the Sunday magazine. Is that really going to help when you're in the off-licence and the review is stuck in the kitchen drawer? Create folders for each subject and be highly selective about what you add.

- Are you addicted to money-off coupons? Do you shove them into your bag and carry them around for months? Only slip those into your purse that you're going to use next time you're at the supermarket.

- Go through all your folders once a year and ditch out-of-date information or anything that you've lost interest in. Now you've got a new sofa you don't need all the homes magazines you bought to inspire you!

'Nothing is as exhausting as indecision and nothing is so futile.'
Bertrand Russell, philosopher

PURGE YOUR PAPERWORK

More and more of us are working from home either full-time or for a day or two each week. Eliminating stressful commuting and smart clothes is a real bonus. Being able to fit work around family life is also a great incentive. But, it also means that the boundaries between home and business get blurred. During the day it can feel as if we're not properly engaged with our job, yet in the evening unfinished projects accuse us from every corner.

## *Activity*

## Create a clearly defined work area

Converting the spare room into a separate office is ideal. But if you're forced to use your living room, then a screen or shelving partition can define your working area. Choose a work station designed to close up at the end of the day and concealed storage so you can reclaim your living space.

### Keep your desk clear

- An uncluttered desk boosts effective concentration.

- Focus on one project at a time and clear your desk at the end of every day.

- Minimise personal items like photos.

- The area under and around the desk should be free of clutter – don't start piling papers and boxes of envelopes on the floor.

### Stay focused

There's always the lure of daytime TV and a million and one domestic jobs like laundry and trips to the dry cleaners to distract you. Don't get sucked into bad habits. Instead, take a lunch break and deal with urgent household matters before returning to your office space.

A downside of working from home is not being able to escape the clutter and chaos anymore. Don't let it have a dampening effect on your whole day – speed tidy for a few minutes before you start work.

**Separate home and work life**

● Have separate filing systems for home and work.

● Get dressed. It feels more professional than slouching around in a frayed dressing gown.

● Walk around the block before you start your working day to get your energy going.

● Use a daily to-do list and don't get distracted by checking your email every five minutes.

● Watch time spent on personal phone calls and texting.

● You're bound to miss the water cooler moments, so schedule meetings outside the home to prevent yourself going stir crazy.

● Decide on a set number of hours that suit your family routine. If you need to work again in the evening, put boundaries around it or you'll feel as though you never get any free time.

PURGE YOUR PAPERWORK

It was predicted that the new millennium would bring a paperless society. It hasn't quite panned out that way. We're working longer hours and suffocating in an avalanche of paper that never seems to stop flowing.

Despite wishful thinking, the paperwork isn't going to magically deal with itself. After your initial surge of enthusiasm, keep up the good work.

## *Activity*

## Win the paper battle in the long term

- Curb your tendency to print a copy of every single article you read online. Bookmark interesting sites so you can revisit them.

- Do it now. Procrastination will quickly lead to paper overload. It only takes a minute or two to file the new mortgage statement or pay the gas bill.

- Stick to the one-minute rule. Your aim is to locate any document in under a minute! Time yourself – if you find it's taking longer, a clearout is overdue.

- Establish a current to-do list in your electronic personal organiser, in your diary or on a sheet of paper on your clipboard. Use it as a daily planning tool.

- Have an action tray for papers that you can't deal with immediately. Go through this at least once a week to make sure nothing's forgotten.

- Create a wishlist folder with cut-outs from papers and magazines. Yes, the cashmere wrap, theatre offer or Thai restaurant look appealing. But only add the most alluring ones to your wishlist folder. Resist the ones you'll never actually use.

- Have an annual blitz where you go through all your folders and have a thorough declutter. Try doing this over a couple of weeks when life is quiet.

- Colour code your folders. That way you can see instantly that the purple box file has last year's tax information.

- Never use scraps of paper to write down essential details like a contact's telephone number. Otherwise you'll end up like Beryl Pfizer...

'I write down everything I want to remember. That way, instead of spending a long time trying to remember what it is I wrote down, I spend the time looking for the paper I wrote it down on.'
Beryl Pfizer, journalist

PURGE YOUR PAPERWORK

# Your notes

# CHAPTER 13

## TAME 21ST CENTURY CLUTTER

In the early 21st century we're surrounded by gizmos designed to make our lives easier, more efficient and pleasurable. But unless you're a gadget lover, the whole process can be exhausting and lead to a muddle of manuals, adapters and wires.

*Activity*

## Control your gizmo glut

Take the two quizzes to gauge your gizmo habits.

**Quiz 1: Are you a gadget lover?**

Score 1 point for each statement you agree with.

● I can't wait to get my hands on the latest gadget.

● I feel embarrassed by out-of-date gadgets and would never use a mobile phone more than a year old.

● I regularly visit stores, online sites and read magazines to see what's happening in the world of electronics.

● I compete with my friends to be the first to get the new, must-have gizmo.

● I love to visit technology shows and exhibitions to check out what's hot.

● I'm always looking for state-of-the-art gadgets to make my life faster and more productive.

**Your score**

If you score three or more, you're hooked on new technology. Clutter problems will arise if you can't bear to part with any of your original gadgets.

### Quiz 2: Gadget clutter quiz

Score 1 point for each statement you agree with.

- When I buy a gizmo like Playstation 2, I hold on to the original Playstation 1.

- It's a struggle to find instruction manuals for any of my equipment.

- I have a lot of plugs, cables, chargers and kit that I can't identify.

- Technology is causing me a lot of stress.

- I have more than one of each of the following (score 1 for each category):
  - mobile phones
  - laptops
  - electronic personal organisers
  - MP3 players.

### Your score

If you score 3 or more, you're in trouble with 21st century clutter.

### TOP TIP

- ◆ Declutter computer games you're bored with. Sell or give away your battle or golf games.
- ◆ Count up how many of each type of gizmo you have. Ben didn't even know he had five laptops – he'd upgraded each year without having any strategy to deal with the older models!
- ◆ Now you've evaluated the gadget overload, tomorrow we'll look at how to make decisive decluttering decisions.

TAME 21ST CENTURY CLUTTER

New technology is upgraded continually and within a few years it's easy to acquire a stash of similar gizmos. Instinctive hoarding seems to prevent gadget lovers from shedding dated equipment even when it's become completely useless.

## Challenge your hoarding fears

Why are you keeping gadgets and gizmos that have been replaced by newer models. Do any of these reasons ring true?

◆ I need a back-up if my current model goes wrong.
◆ There's personal data on the phone or computer.
◆ I spent a lot of money on the old version and I don't want to waste it.
◆ I would give it away but I can't find all the attachments.
◆ The gizmo is broken and I keep meaning to get it repaired.
◆ These gadgets will be collector's items in 20 years.

## Be honest

If you drop your mobile phone are you likely to:

a) re-use an old model from your hoard?
b) hotfoot it round to the shop and get the one that's just been launched?

If the answer is b) then why have you still got four old phones? Don't cling on to stuff you won't use again even if it was expensive. Unless it's a recent model, the resale value will be limited.

*Activity*

## Unscramble your gadgets

- Don't toss old equipment. There are charities that will recycle computers and mobiles (see the further reading section at the back of this book).

- Get a box and collect up all the attachments and cables. Use your investigative skills to re-unite them with the gadget they belong to. In future, stick parts you rarely use into a transparent bag with a description, or label with a permanent marker.

- Set up a box file to keep all manuals for technology products together.

- Always use the one in, one out policy. When you buy a new electronic organiser, hand on or sell the old one straight away. Consult the owner's manual on how to delete personal information.

- With technology, if you haven't used it in the last year it's unlikely you'll pick it up again. So use the 'one-year rule' as a guideline.

Your computer will take up the same amount of physical space whether your inbox is clogged with hundreds of emails or kept under control. Emails are a fantastic way to communicate but can take up vast tracts of time and, often, very little of it is constructive!

## *Activity*

## Examine your email habits

You either love emails or they drive you crazy. See how they're affecting you by taking the email quiz. Score 1 point for each statement you agree with.

- I feel obliged to answer all emails at once.

- I can't resist reading junk emails.

- I have 100s of emails in my inbox.

- I don't have a system for filing emails that I need for reference.

- I'm always printing out copies of emails.

- I never go back through folders and delete old emails.

- I waste a lot of time looking at emails when I have more important priorities.

### Your score

If you scored three or more, your email habits will be contributing to mental clutter and a feeling of constant pressure.

### Grab control

Your immediate goal is to go through your inbox and delete as much junk as possible. Remember you don't have to read marketing material!

**TOP TIP**

- Don't think that you have to respond to all emails straight away. Differentiate between emails that need urgent attention and interesting newsletters that can wait until you have some down time.
- Only look at your inbox at specific times during the day.
- Set up folders to store significant emails for future reference. Use a similar system to your paper filing to keep things coherent.
- Turn your computer off in the evening so you're not tempted to sneak back and start faffing with emails.
- Have at least one computer-free day a week when you leave it switched off. Although the culture with mobile phones and emails is to be available 24 hours a day, this is a direct route to a cluttered mind.
- Have a policy about deleting emails. I keep mine for a month and then get rid of the lot.
- Install a spam filter so less junk ends up in your inbox.
- Never open attachments from strangers or divulge personal financial details. Your bank or building society would never request this information by email.
- Use your inbox in a similar way to your action tray – only leave emails here that need further attention.

'To err is human, but to really foul things up requires a computer.'
Farmers' Almanac

TAME 21ST CENTURY CLUTTER

# Your notes

# CHAPTER 14

## UNLOAD
## UNWANTED STUFF

This chapter explores the diverse ways we can offload our unwanted stuff. It's easier to say goodbye to our surplus possessions if we know they're going to a find a new owner, raise some cash or be recycled into something brand new. You'll find resources for all these avenues in the further information section at the back of the book.

## Win, win, win

Donating to charity is win, win, win, all the way!

◆ You win because you end up with less stuff and a positive feeling that you're helping others.
◆ The new owner wins because they get a bargain for a few pounds.
◆ The charity wins because it raises much-needed funds.

*Activity*

## Delight in donating to charity

Here are some suggestions to smooth the process of giving to charity:

**Charity shops**

● Support a charity shop whose aims and values are important to you.

● They want quality things to sell so donate clean items in good condition.

● Check whether local charities offer collection. Do book in advance as they have heavy demands on their volunteers' time.

● If you leave donated goods on the doorsteps of charity shops overnight, they're likely to be stolen. Take your bags during opening hours.

- Furniture or electrical equipment must meet strict safety regulations to be resold. Most charity shops don't accept them but they probably know a project that refurbishes furniture, computers and other household appliances.

### Community organisations

Nurseries, toy libraries, after-school clubs and youth groups are run on a shoestring, so why not give your craft materials or excess games and toys directly to them?

- Schools and libraries usually accept donations of books.

- Charities that work with homeless people, like Crisis, need a wide range of things throughout the year.

- Animal sanctuaries welcome pet baskets, blankets, toys and cans of unopened pet food.

### Online resources

There are a growing number of websites where you can offer your goods free to charities and community groups.

You'll also find exciting ethical gifts these days from charitable websites – giving a chicken or planting a tree is a brilliant, clutter-free present.

### Buying from charity

I buy novels and videos from charity shops, read or watch them and then take them straight back. It's a kind of charitable lending library for me!

UNLOAD UNWANTED STUFF

TV programmes incessantly urge us to turn our clutter into cash. Yet there's a world of difference between chucking something in the spare room with the vague idea of selling it and actually taking it round to the designer dress shop or advertising on eBay.

Selling only succeeds if you get organised and dedicate the time.

## Car boot sales

Car boot sales are good if you have lots of low-cost items to sell at once. You'll need time to prepare for the sale, a free day at the week-end, storage capacity and transport. Get a friend to share your pitch so you can grab a cup of tea or pop to the loo.

Don't start filling the garage sky-high in January if you can't do a boot sale until October. Decide the date and venue of the sale in advance. After it's over, take decent things to the charity shop, rubbish to the tip and nothing home!

## Auctions

TV programmes like *Bargain Hunt* have demystified the process of selling at auction. So if you have collectables, antiques or period furniture, discuss a valuation with your local auction house. Check what commission, transport and insurance costs they charge.

If you decide to sell antiques through a dealer, contact the Association of Art and Antique Dealers to find a reputable one.

## Second-hand shops

Designer clothes, antiques or LPs can be sold through second-hand or specialist shops. Check the shop's policy on whether they buy outright or give you a percentage after the sale.

House-clearance firms had a dodgy reputation in the past. Do ask around for a recommendation if you have to clear a lot of possessions quickly.

UNLOAD UNWANTED STUFF

## Local advertising

Local papers often offer free adverts. Or use the traditional method of placing a postcard in the newsagent's window. It's low cost and will reach local buyers, which is ideal for bulky items like furniture.

## Selling online

The internet is the 21st century way to sell everything. As well as the big players like eBay and Amazon, do some searching and you'll be amazed at the range of sites out there. If you find the idea of placing an ad on eBay a drag, there are agents who will sell your stuff for a fee.

But don't get addicted to browsing and buy more than you sell. Remember, you're aiming to unload clutter, not acquire more!

*Activity*

## Make definite plans for selling good quality possessions

If you're keen on recouping some of the cash you've spent, put your selling strategy into action.

**Do**

- Be realistic about the value of second-hand goods. Unless you have antiques, collectables or designer clothing, it's unlikely that you'll get rich.

- Plan a special treat from the proceeds. The thought of a pampering day or new boots will motivate you to get going!

- Choose the best method for selling your surplus.

UNLOAD UNWANTED STUFF

There's so much more to recycling that taking newspapers, glass bottles and tin cans to the local recycling centre or putting them in your kerbside box. Many seemingly useless items can be reincarnated through recycling. Before you dump your printer, glasses, cardboard boxes, old blankets, cans of paint, shoes, bicycles or mobile phones, investigate recycling possibilities.

 TOP TIP

- Don't feel it's too much hassle to recycle. It does take a little longer than binning something but it means that you have the satisfaction of knowing that you're minimising waste and the pressure on landfill sites.
- Never bin mobile phones or toner cartridges. Give them to charities that can make money from recycling them.

*Activity*

# Be resourceful in your recycling

- Phone your council or search online to find out what's available in your local area. My local council Barnet is one of the first in the UK to introduce compulsory recycling, which works incredibly well – you get a fine if you don't recycle! They also have a green bin for garden and food scraps to make into compost.

- Compost heaps are a brilliant way to turn scraps into nourishment for the garden. Even a small one will be a good place for all the peelings, dead flowers and coffee grounds. You can also add paper from your shredder.

- Wherever possible, buy goods with the minimum of packaging. Don't automatically accept a carrier bag but, if you do, re-use it for shopping or turn it into a bin-liner.

- If you live in an urban area try the 'take me' approach to recycling bulky, low-value items that can still be used, like a chair or a metal bookcase. Put it outside your home with a notice saying 'please take me'. Chances are that someone will whisk it away so it can have a new lease of life.

- Question our disposable society where things last a year or two and then fall apart. Wherever possible, buy quality articles that will last. Get a decent suitcase rather than a cheapie with a zip that breaks the second time you use it.

UNLOAD UNWANTED STUFF

In an ideal world there would be minimal waste and our bins would be virtually empty. We'd be recycling, donating and re-using whatever we could. Being brought up by parents who grew up in the Second World War I hate waste. But I also hate clutter and I've had to come to terms with the fact that there are currently some things that we don't have the resources to recycle.

## Do

♦ Accept that even with all your good intentions there will still be things you have to chuck like broken hairdryers, a jigsaw with half the pieces missing or smashed up kids' toys.
♦ Ensure that all rubbish has been binned at the end of each decluttering session.
♦ Empty your waste bins daily. Feng Shui practitioners believe this helps to maintain good energy in our homes.
♦ Use a skip if clutter really has got the upper hand in your garage or garden.
♦ Local councils will collect bulky rubbish like old mattresses. Check if there's a charge and how many items are included in the fee.

## Don't

♦ Never bin toxic chemicals. Your council information office will advise on safe disposal of paint, batteries (including car batteries) and chemicals used for the garden or DIY.
♦ Don't put junk in the loft, garage or hallway and then relax and forget about it. Leaving it for weeks in the driveway will be a real eyesore and will annoy your neighbours. As soon as you know something is trash, get it off your property as quickly as possible.

# Activity

## Learn to recognise rubbish and chuck it

Scoot round and identify five objects that are pure trash. If they can't be recycled, then fling them in the bin with relish. They're junk and they don't belong in your home!

### TOP TIP

Freeing your home from dross on a daily basis is incredibly liberating. Without a layer of clutter, you'll be able to see its true beauty and potential.

When we lend our hedge trimmer to a neighbour it leaves a bad taste in the mouth if six months later, they've still got it! Years ago I had a great collection of blues LPs, which I lent to a friend's boyfriend. When they split up I asked for them back but he drifted out of my life without returning them. I felt my initial generosity had been taken for granted and exploited.

## Long-term strategies

◆ If you have a bad record of returning items, either stop borrowing altogether or make a note on the calendar to take things back by a set date. Tell your friend to remind you in a couple of weeks so they don't feel like a nag.

◆ If you always end up paying fines on overdue library books and DVDs, make a note in your diary when they're due back. Once you're finished with them, put them in a visible spot to jog your memory.

◆ Don't feel you have to lend things just because someone asks. If your sister always keeps your books, in future only pass on those you don't want anymore.

### *Activity*

## Check your progress

How's it going with your paperwork? Have a quick look back at Day 71 to refresh your memory about good paper habits. Are you managing to implement most of them? Well done! Spend a couple of minutes updating your to-do list and making sure that there's no unopened post, shredding or late bills to be dealt with.

*Activity*

# Mend fences by returning borrowed things

Do you feel guilty when you come across an evening bag or a sander you borrowed ages ago? Had you totally forgotten about it?

- 'Fess up and return it. Acknowledge your slip by accompanying it with a bottle of wine or box of chocolates.

- If you've broken or lost someone's belongings and then felt too awful to tell them, don't let it ruin a friendship. Admit what's happened and offer to replace the item or refund its value.

- Occasionally you'll come across things that belong to people you're out of touch with. Lou had a faded suit belonging to a college friend he'd lost track of. It was a tough call but he let it go. Doing this never feels particularly good, so always return everything promptly.

- If someone has your belongings, you're perfectly entitled to ask for them back. Why should you waste your money buying another electric screwdriver?

- If you decide to declutter the pressure cooker your friend borrowed months ago and never returned, then tell her it's now hers. That way any tension will dissipate!

'Who goes a borrowing
Goeth a sorrowing.
Few lendeth (but fools)
Their working tools.'
Thomas Tusser, 16th century
farmer and poet

UNLOAD UNWANTED STUFF

185

Re-gifting can be a great way to hand superfluous things on to friends or family. If you're given a body lotion you don't like, either offer it to someone you know or add to your present box to 're-gift' at a future date.

---

### CASE STUDY

Maggie had embraced cheap chic in a big way. She was brilliant at discovering brand-new clothes in charity shops. Yet since she'd dropped two dress sizes at a slimming club, she was faced with a wardrobe full of oversized clothes.

She invited over a group of weight-watching friends who brought along clothes that didn't fit any more. Over a glass of wine they had fun trying things on and managed to replenish their wardrobes for free. It was a smart way to celebrate their weight loss and rid themselves of cluttered closets!

---

## Swapping sessions

Get together with colleagues or friends for a swapping session. You can exchange a bottle of aftershave for a computer game or have a laugh modelling each other's clothes. This works well for parents of young children – swapping baby gear for toddler equipment.

Free treats are appealing – but be discriminating. Remember, it costs nothing in money terms but it's going to cost you space in your home!

## Online resources

There are a growing number of sites where you can swap your goods online. Your surplus second car vacuum cleaner can be switched for a record player!

UNLOAD UNWANTED STUFF

*Activity*

# Regifting dos and don'ts

## Do

- If your mum or best friend might fancy your velvet curtains or travel iron, ask them today if they're interested or arrange lunch soon so they can have a look.

- Accept that it's not always possible for your belongings to go to someone close. Until recently things were passed things down through the generations. But life has changed, so if no-one in the family wants your great-grandmother's tea service, then sell it without remorse.

## Don't

- Don't overload friends and family. Always give them a choice whether to take your cast-offs or not. It's better to say no politely than to accept something that ends up as clutter.

- Don't use re-gifting as an unconscious way of holding on to possessions. The garden statue you gave to your sister now belongs to her. She's free to decide its fate.

- Never forget who the gift was from and give it back to them. Imagine the family fight *that* would spark! So if you've got a dicey memory, make a note of the original giver.

- Don't feel mean because you're passing on gifts you didn't buy. We all have times when we're broke or too busy to go shopping.

UNLOAD UNWANTED STUFF

**187**

# Your notes

# CHAPTER 15

## SELECT STYLISH STORAGE

The *Chambers 21st Century Dictionary* defines 'put something into storage' as 'to put it away temporarily until it is needed again.'

The words 'temporarily' and 'needed' are the key ones here. The purpose of storage is to make things easy to find and to keep them in good shape. Storage is not for keeping something you don't need forever!

## *Activity*

## Sidestep storage traps

Spend a few minutes considering:

- one area in your home where the storage is spot on. Perhaps you've cracked it in the bathroom with a corner cupboard and a large bathroom cabinet

- another area where there's a never-ending struggle with disorder, like the hallway.

Analyse what's working so well in the first area and any lessons you could apply to the untidy zone.

## TOP TIP

If you're tearing your hair out with frustration at the mess and muddle, a carload of seductive storage products looks like the solution. But before you rush to the shops, be careful that your boxes and containers don't become even more clutter!

◆ Buying storage before you've decluttered is the wrong way around. Until you've pared down your possessions, you won't know what you need. If you buy 100 hangers you may find that you only need 60. The others will be chucked in the bottom of the wardrobe, wasting space and money.

◆ Never buy storage products just because they look great. Decide first exactly what you're going to do with them and if they're the right size for the job.

◆ Multi-buys, like a set of different-sized boxes, appear good value – but not if only a couple of the boxes are useful.

◆ Overfilling drawers and cupboards is a true clutter trap. Ditch the notion that you have to pack everything to bursting point.

SELECT STYLISH STORAGE

'A place for everything and everything in its place' has been a useful mantra since the 17th century. Don't reject this basic notion because you're afraid of becoming obsessive. There's a big difference between finding the new shampoo or AA batteries without a hullabaloo and turning into someone who can't bear to see a stray glass or a rumpled cushion!

## *Activity*

# Sign up for successful storage habits

Grab a laundry basket, go from room to room collecting anything that's in the wrong place, and return it to its proper home.

### Select the best storage spot

If you come across things that don't belong anywhere, resist the temptation to shove them in the first room you come across. Take a minute to find the most appropriate place to keep them. If you use something regularly, choose a hot spot, but if it's only used once in a blue moon, then select a cold storage spot.

### *Hotspots*

Hotspots are choice places ideal for your most frequently used things. For example, locate your spatula, oven gloves and cooking oil close to the cooker.

### *Cold spots*

Cold spots are hard-to-reach cupboards or high-up shelves – best for storing a sleeping bag or the Mah jong set you only get out twice a year.

### *VITs*

Cindy Glovinsky coined the term 'very important things' or VITs for crucial documents like insurance policies and bits of kit like car keys. If you lose VITs there's going to be a lot of wasted time and frustration. Don't be like Jackie who was in such chaos that she had to cancel her holiday after an extensive hunt failed to unearth her passport!

VITs need easily-accessed storage. It's fine to use a secret place as long as you keep this consistent. How many times have you come back from a trip and found that you can't remember where you hid your cashcards or the back-door key?

## In future

◆ Spend five minutes a day, either morning or evening, zooming round and rehoming stuff.
◆ Always clear files and projects away at the end of a working day to leave your desk clutter free.
◆ Get your kids into a daily routine of tidying away their toys or computer games.

If you're constantly running up and down stairs, use a stair basket to temporarily hold things. Then you can grab it next time you're on your way up.

## ⊙ TOP TIP

When contemplating buying a smoothie maker or yet another power tool, consider storage. Visualise exactly where you're going to keep it. If it's a larger item like an electric piano, take measurements and see if it will fit in the available space.

SELECT STYLISH STORAGE

Life's too short to waste time racking your brain or second-guessing where your spare key or swimming goggles are. Applying basic storage principles will make home life much easier to manage.

## *Activity*
# Simplify your storage

**Store like with like**

- Group all similar items, like batteries, in one place.

- Collect together things you habitually use at the same time, like envelopes, birthday cards and stamps.

- Choose an appropriate storage container for each cluster. A tin holding your shoe polish, suede sprays and shoelaces will mean less faffing about when you've got an important meeting and your shoes are scuffed.

- If your headache tablets are always on the top shelf of the bathroom cabinet, you'll know straight away when you're going to run out. That'll trigger you to get some replacements before a Sunday-evening migraine strikes.

- If you live in a Georgian townhouse with lots of different floors, you won't want to run downstairs every time you need a pair of scissors. Keep a stash of basic supplies in different areas of your house.

**Colour code your storage**

- A shortcut to finding things speedily is to use colour coding throughout your home. The blue jar holds the English breakfast tea and the grey one has the camomile teabags. This will help the whole household – it's so much easier to say it's in the green box than it's the third box on the right.

- If you prefer things less colourful, use transparent shoe boxes or glass jars so you can see the contents.

## Use labels

At the beginning of December do you wonder where you put the Christmas decorations? It's unrealistic to expect yourself to remember off the top of your head where everything is stored. A labelled box is going to be a lot quicker to unearth in the loft or hall cupboard.

## Record where things are stored

Use a card index as a record of storage and update this regularly. Life will be easier if you keep the decorations in the same spot every year. But don't signal to burglars where your valuables are – make coded records of where your jewellery and share certificates are stashed.

## TOP TIP

If you've been disorganised in the past you'll have squandered many hours searching for lost stuff. Aim for the one-minute rule: it should take under a minute to find objects or papers. Even if you achieve this 80 per cent of the time, think how much aggravation you'll avoid!

SELECT STYLISH STORAGE

DAY 84: STORAGE PRODUCTS

Buying attractive storage products will add organization, style and glamour to your home.

- Expect high standards from storage products. Always try out drawers and lids to see how easy they are to use. Many products look good but are shabbily made. You want storage to be attractive and function efficiently.
- Splash out on storage products that are going to be on display like your memory box. If you're going to store things in kitchen drawers, you can use ice-cream cartons or even the plastic cartons from fruit to subdivide marker pens from freezer labels.
- Think dual function when you choose furniture. Integral underbed drawers can contain clean bedlinen or out-of-season clothing. A coffee table with a shelf can hold newspapers and magazines.
- Aim for easy retrieval. A deep chest may seem ideal for toys, but if your toddler has to chuck everything out onto the floor to find the tractor at the bottom, it's not going to work very well.
- Choose concealed storage if you struggle to fold towels neatly or if you prefer the clean, uncluttered lines achieved with most of your possessions out of sight.
- Stay up to date with innovations in storage design. If you've hankered after a new kitchen or fitted wardrobe recently, you've probably found all the new storage tricks inspiring. Even if you can't afford it at the moment, choose one great idea or product to improve your storage.
- Commission built-in floor-to-ceiling storage to maximise the space available. This will mean that you can take advantage of irregular areas, like the corners of rooms and alcoves. Make sure you always include lighting in your plans.

## Activity
# Sex up your storage

Take a trip round the shops to look at the range of storage solutions on offer. Find inspiration as well by browsing online or in catalogues. But don't spend any money today – just look in an open-minded way. Jot down the most appealing and then imagine them fitting in with your decor. Once you've narrowed down the shortlist, treat yourself.

SELECT STYLISH STORAGE

# Your notes

# CHAPTER 16

# STEM THE TIDE
# OF STUFF

There's no clutter genie who visits in the night and deposits objects throughout your home. Apart from the post or presents, things can only enter if you or one of your household brings them in. Many people find this hard to accept when faced with a mystery object that doesn't appear to belong to them.

## ◎━◄ TOP TIP

- It doesn't matter whether a jug costs 50p or £500 – what counts is how much you like it.
- Beware of the false belief that if it's good value, it somehow won't become clutter. Cheap and even free stuff always comes with a hidden cost – it will take up space in your home.
- If over-generous relations shower your child with presents each time they visit or bring you strange family heirlooms you don't want, tell them politely that you're streamlining your life.

## Clutter cycle

Nowadays there's always something new and exciting to tempt us. But the quest for amassing endless possessions will eventually lead to stretched finances and a jumbled home. There's also the law of diminishing returns – the more we have, the less we value it. As our satisfaction drops, we crave something new to give us a lift. In this way the clutter cycle perpetuates itself.

'You can't have everything. Where would you put it?' Steven Wright, US comedian and actor

*Activity*

## Unravel the mystery of how possessions arrive at your home

Over the next few days we're going to look at your shopping habits and your magpie tendencies. In the meantime, consider whether your relationship with material things has gone off the rails. Do you believe the consumer myth that you can never have too much stuff?

If you're bringing in new goods faster than you can mentally catalogue them or form any kind of attachment, decelerate the process. A fundamental concept in staying clutter free is monitoring the flow of stuff in.

Before acquiring anything new, ask some key questions:

● Do I need it?

● Do I already have similar or identical items?

● Do I have room to store it?

● Can I afford it?

● What will I do with it when I don't use it anymore?

● Is it exactly what I want?

● If I didn't buy it, how much would it bother me in a week's time?

STEM THE TIDE OF STUFF

Recent research by Dr Dennis from Brunel University has found significant differences in the way men and women approach shopping. Men use their 'hunter-gatherer' skills to focus on bagging desired items quickly and efficiently. Women, on the other hand, see shopping as a leisure activity: they spend longer and visit many more shops per trip.

## *Activity*

## Review your retail therapy

Think back over the last couple of weeks and write down everything you've bought apart from food. Refresh your memory by digging receipts out of your bag or wallet. Once you've made the list, make a note at the side of each item:

● Was it something you needed?

● Was it an impulse buy?

● Are you pleased with it?

● What mood were you in when you bought it?

● Have you used it or worn it yet?

If you've been shopping non-stop or treating yourself when you're stressed, it's time to break the cycle of overbuying.

'Most men hate to shop. That's why the men's department is usually on the first floor of a department store, two inches from the door.'
John Wayne, actor

**TOP TIP**

- At least one weekend a month, have a shopping-free zone. Choose another activity – visit a gallery, spend the afternoon at the cinema or, if money's tight, go for a long walk.
- If you're upset or angry, restrict retail therapy to a small treat like a CD, DVD or a lipstick.
- Choose quality over quantity. Buy one great fitting pair of jeans rather than several cut-price versions.
- Don't settle for 'good enough' – aim for amazing. Michael Willmot's research from the Future Foundation has shown that 50 per cent of shoppers don't worry about getting the best result. He sees this complacency as a symptom of our throw-away culture.
- If compulsive shopping is leading you into financial trouble, set yourself a weekly budget and only use cash.
- Online shopping, catalogues or TV shopping channels may not feel like spending real money but your credit card bills will tell a different story.
- Beware bargains. The shopping fever that takes hold during the sales allows stores to move incredible junk. Don't clog your home up with more clutter!
- *Prima* magazine found that half of women regularly return their purchases to the shops. If a chronic cycle of buying and taking things back develops, this is known as shopping bulimia.
- Shopping addiction is often treated as a joke, but it can become a serious problem. If you're shopping every day, buying stuff you can't afford, and hiding bags and receipts from yourself and your partner, consider seeking professional help.

STEM THE TIDE OF STUFF

'Magpies' are irresistibly drawn to anything and everything they can find. They can get the same buzz rescuing a friend's discarded deckchair, ferreting out a bargain at the local car boot sale or spotting a three-for-two bargain on pink paper. It doesn't bother them that they never use pink paper or don't have a garden. A bargain is a bargain and the more the merrier! Highly creative magpie-types are optimists who believe that, one day, pink paper will come in useful. They've spent little money to turn their homes into Aladdin's caves of clutter.

## TOP TIP

- ◆ Take a breath and reflect carefully before you automatically say yes to a free offer.
- ◆ Go to a car boot sale or the shops with enough money for a cup of tea and see how it feels to enjoy looking but buy nothing.
- ◆ Accept that not everything will be useful to you. Pass your clutter on today to someone who will use it.
- ◆ For everything new you acquire, let one comparable object go. That'll make you think twice before getting another cushion or screwdriver.

STEM THE TIDE OF STUFF

*Activity*

# Are you a magpie hoarder?

Score 1 for every 'yes':

- If someone offers you something, do you always take it?

- Do you buy junk you don't need at the sales because it's so cheap?

- Do you love to rummage for bargains at charity shops and car boot sales?

- Do you need to be surrounded by a lot of stuff?

- Do you feel attached to all your possessions and find it tough to part with anything?

- Do you have more than one collection on the go?

- No matter how many shoes or towels you own, do you still want more?

- Do you accumulate things like fancy dress outfits because they might be useful to friends and family?

**Your score**

0–2: Minimal magpie leanings

3–8: You're a magpie hoarder!

Everything you own has a cost. As well as the financial cost, it will take up space in your home. It will also require attention – cleaning, mending and insuring. It's easy to become overwhelmed, physically and mentally. Possessions no longer bring you pleasure – they feel more like a weighty burden. You find yourself fantasising about living on a desert island free from clutter.

## Treat or tat?

Understand how enticing displays look in shops. When you're tempted by something pretty or yet another gizmo, ask yourself, 'Is it worth buying or is just more stuff?' One definition of stuff is 'useless objects'!

### TOP TIP

- ◆ Refuse politely to accept unwanted cast-offs from well-meaning friends and family members. This will help to stem the flow of clutter into your home.
- ◆ Don't store other people's junk, even if it's in your garage or loft. The original few weeks can easily turn into months and years. If you're already looking after someone's possessions, give them a deadline to pick it all up. That includes your grown-up kids who have places of their own but still think you want a loft full of their childhood trappings.
- ◆ Flora had got into a rut of buying useless souvenirs on cruise holidays because everyone else did! Her bungalow was overcrowded with these tacky, unloved mementos. She finally learned to say no to pointless acquisitions and came back from her latest holiday with only a key ring! Next time you take a weekend break or visit a museum, feel empowered to return without a memento.

*Activity*

## Become more aware of how you accumulate stuff

● Make people aware of your desire for a simpler lifestyle. That way you can agree to stop exchanging holiday or Christmas presents. Stick to birthday gifts and a great night out at New Year.

● Understand that if you've been searching for something for a while, it's common for the desire to linger. I bought myself a digital radio recently, yet find myself still staring at radios in shop windows. If you're not on your guard, you'll come home with an unneeded duplicate.

● Wanting things can be a passing fad for adults as well as kids. Don't rush out and buy something the minute it occurs to you. See if you're as keen in a week's time.

● Keep a wishlist for treats you fancy. It's great to pull this out when you're having a rough time or to reward yourself for finishing a project.

'You can only have so many pairs of shoes and then you go, "Well I've got enough shoes what else can I do?" ' Oprah Winfrey, US TV chat show host

# Your notes

# CHAPTER 17

## NURTURE
## NEW HABITS

Once clutter is no longer bulging out of every nook and cranny, how do you keep things this way? This chapter explores key habits that will help you stay clutter free.

One in, one out is straightforward. For every item that you bring into your home, you let a similar one go. That includes second-hand and free stuff as well.

Here are some examples:

♦ You get a new TV licence – immediately shred the previous one.
♦ You buy a new dressing gown – give the old one to charity.
♦ Today's newspaper comes – yesterday's goes to the recycling.
♦ A multipack of six pairs of socks replaces six shabby ones.
♦ You're given a new digital radio – donate your FM one.

You get the idea!

## *Activity* Check your recent acquisitions

Cast your mind back over everything you've acquired in the past month. If your mind has gone blank, check your last bank statement or credit card bill. Did you adopt the one in, one out principle? If not, retrace your steps and do it now.

And remember, if you're not ready to part with your existing gym bag or kitchen clock yet, then there's no need to buy a new one!

### TOP TIP

♦ Even though the hairdryer is bust, do you feel a weird attachment to it? Rather than bin it, do you stick it in the garage for that mythical day when it will miraculously become intact again? Accept that some things can't be mended so bin or recycle them straight away.

Procrastination goes hand in hand with hoarding. We've all heard the famous quotation by Edward Young that 'procrastination is the thief of time'. Procrastination is also the enemy of order and leads to a muddled head and a messy home. Yet the voice that says, 'I really will sort out my bedroom – tomorrow,' is seductive and often hard to overcome.

## Don't be afraid of making a mistake

If you continually put off dealing with something, then you're holding on to it. Sure, you don't miss your stamp collection but you're still left dangling. You don't get the cathartic pleasure of knowing you've completed a task and made progress. Neither do you get the blissful feeling of creating clear space and a clear mind.

*Activity*

## Say goodbye to procrastination

Focus on a task you've been avoiding for a few days – it might be answering a tricky email, sewing a button on your shirt or taking a bag to the charity shop. It won't disappear even if you dither, so do it now rather than waste time worrying.

When it's done and dusted, consider whether it was as hard work as you'd anticipated. It probably wasn't, was it? We all have a tendency to overestimate chores we find unpalatable.

### ◎ ⚡ TOP TIP

- Tackle thorny jobs first thing in the morning – that way they won't hang over you all day.
- Lifelong procrastinators will have to be vigilant. If you notice you're postponing one particular task again and again, then add it to the top of your to-do list and do it at the first opportunity.
- Watch out for perfectionism. Perhaps you're scared that even after you've finished doing up a room it still won't be up to scratch. Real homes rarely resemble the glossy magazines!
- Break each area down into manageable segments – like a shelf at a time.
- Sometimes tasks have to be deferred. If you've been ill or have a demanding report to write, leave the loft until the pressure has lifted. Make a note in your diary a month or two ahead to remind yourself that the work is outstanding.

'Remember that fear always lurks behind perfectionism. Confronting your fears and allowing yourself the right to be human can, paradoxically, make you a far happier and more productive person.' Dr David M. Burns, psychiatrist

NURTURE NEW HABITS

Do you like to squirrel away your prize property for safekeeping? Have you only used your dinner service or worn your expensive watch a handful of times? Are you slouching around in shabby slippers when you have two pristine pairs in your cupboard?

People often mistakenly believe that decluttering is a kind of deprivation – it means losing possessions you value. The opposite is true – you only keep things you treasure and love using. You're no longer a custodian of your worldly goods, preserving things for future generations. You're free to luxuriate in lovely things!

## The dilemma of using things

- **Downside:** Things in use will get worn down over time. They may possibly break or get lost and may need to be replaced.
- **Upside:** If you use something opulent, you'll pamper yourself and revel in the feeling that you're worth it. You may even get compliments. All this will do wonders for your mood and your self-esteem.

## Guilt

The *Chambers 21st Century Dictionary* defines guilt as 'a feeling of shame or remorse resulting from a sense of having done wrong'.

It's hard to enjoy your belongings or indeed feel entitled to them if you're drowning in guilt. These days consumer goods are designed to last a few years or to be rapidly overtaken by new models and faster technology. Despite this, many of us feel that our relationship with possessions should be a long one, perhaps even a lifelong union.

If you're struggling to use the 'good stuff', are any of these beliefs hampering your enjoyment? Do you think you must:

- ◆ make do and mend?
- ◆ save the best china or towels for visitors and guests?
- ◆ be frugal and get your money's worth out of older stuff before using the new?
- ◆ pass on your material goods to the next generation?
- ◆ beat yourself up if you break something?
- ◆ never chuck anything away even if it's broken?

Change your mindset. Give yourself permission to find good homes for unwanted older stuff and to really enjoy your fabulous possessions.

*Activity*

## Enjoy your things

Resolve from now on that possessions will enhance your life.

Ferret out one thing you've been saving and use it today just for the sheer personal pleasure – whether it's the duvet cover still in its wrapper, a china cup for your tea, a stunning piece of jewellery or even a tin of expensive soup. Does it feel illicit? Do you feel guilty or do you feel a real sense of satisfaction?

### TOP TIP

Keep this mantra in mind: 'This is my life – these are my possessions – I am free to do with them as I will!'

You deserve to enjoy your life and home. Surrounding yourself with belongings that have positive associations and bring back happy memories will help you meet this goal.

## Hoarding hang-ups

Dumping things that make you unhappy seems obvious and easily achieved, but it can be more complicated. It's easy to be influenced by external factors and find yourself wavering.

Here are some of the reasons:

◆ It was a gift or inherited.
◆ It was expensive.
◆ You've had it for ages.
◆ Your partner or friends like it.
◆ It's got a lot of wear in it yet.

Even if all these are true, so what? It's upsetting you and that's all you need to know. Letting go of these negative memories will feel so liberating. You're saying to yourself that you deserve better now and in the future.

*Activity*

# Keep possessions that make you happy

Use the smile test to help you decide what to keep and what to discard.

I opened up my Christmas box and the minute I saw the Bloomingdale's bag I started smiling. Being reunited with the baubles and fairy I brought back from New York was a real pleasure. I'd forgotten buying them and was immediately taken back to a fantastic holiday and a snowy Central Park. Unquestionably, they had passed the smile test.

Today, spend ten minutes decluttering photos, holiday souvenirs, cards or any other collection that you've amassed.

As you look at each item, gauge your emotional reaction. Do you feel happy? Do you feel like breaking into a grin? If so, you've come across true treasure that you will want to keep.

### Unhappy memories

All of us have ups and downs in our lives. There are times when life kicks us in the teeth – we lose our job, our partner leaves or we have serious health problems. Certain objects become identified with these miserable periods and every time we see them, we're dragged back.

- Possessions that remind us of traumatic episodes certainly won't pass the smile test. The best strategy is to get rid of them.

- Get things with troubled associations out of the house. Give them to a charity shop further afield so you never have to come across them again!

- If personal letters or photos are depressing, you might choose to rip them up or burn them!

NURTURE NEW HABITS

The more interesting you make decluttering, the easier it will be. You're aiming to turn it from a chore into a challenge!

## Activity

### Set daily decluttering challenges

Try one of these fun methods today. Over the coming weeks choose one every day to keep your motivation high.

- Roll the dice. If you get a 4, then your task today is to declutter four things.

- Choose a number. Three is a good one and for a week get rid of three things a day. That's 21 by the end of the week!

- Use a timer and see how fast you can fill a bag for charity or the rubbish bin.

- Put on an uplifting CD and see what you can achieve by the time it finishes. It's worth doing this even to a single track if you're busy.

- If you always watch *Coronation Street*, then ten minutes beforehand open your post or clear out your fridge. It'll be easy because you know your reward is coming.

- Bribe yourself. You want a new pair of boots or a sleeker mobile phone. Well you can have what you want after you take one binliner to the charity shop.

- Have a go at selling on one of the online auction sites like eBay. No matter how little money is involved, the last few minutes before an auction closes are exciting.

- Shred and rip paper. This can be invigorating, especially when you're in a bad mood. Jumping up and down on cardboard boxes is great fun too!

- Did you ever play the memory game at childhood parties, where you were quickly shown a tray and when it was taken away you had to remember all the objects on it. Well, close your eyes and see if you can remember exactly what's in one of your drawers. It's as good as counting sheep if you can't sleep!

NURTURE NEW HABITS

Everyone gets attached to possessions – they become part of our lives and identity so it can be sad to say goodbye. But if this sentimentality got the upper hand, we'd never relinquish anything. Instead of trusting our feelings, we allow external factors like cost or someone else's opinion to sway us.

## Go with your gut feelings

The last time you had a real mental tussle about giving something away, did your nerve fail you? Did it mean that you kept something that deep down you knew was clutter?

The sequence of events probably went something like this:

You pick up a black cardigan. Your first instinct is to give it to charity – after all it's become slightly tatty. But as you drop it into the charity bag you feel uncomfortable and doubts start to emerge:

◆ It cost £70 and you've only worn it for one winter (even though you wore it nearly every day!)
◆ You received lots of compliments when you first bought it.
◆ You worry this season's version won't be as versatile.
◆ You really loved it – maybe it isn't as timeworn as you first thought.

So your hand hovers over the charity bag and out it comes! Does that sound familiar? This failure of resolve and courage is incredibly common. Avoid it in future by applying the following tips.

NURTURE NEW HABITS

*Activity*

## Helpful hints

- Get used to trusting your first reaction – it's the most honest one.

- Accept that possessions flow through our lives.

- Don't get hung up on the money you spent. It's gone now and even if you sell something, you can only bring a bit of it back.

- If you're dithering, put the item aside for a few days. If you really want to keep it, then it will call you back. You'll wake up at 3 am thinking, 'I do want that necklace.'

- The sooner you take stuff to the charity shop, the less time you have to revisit all your decisions.

- If you ask other people's opinions, you'll get even more confused. Learn to make your own decluttering choices.

- Don't obsess about making a mistake you'll come to regret. Of course it will happen occasionally. But that's life and you'll cope. Focus instead on the dozens of things you discarded and never missed!

'Creativity comes from trust. Trust your instincts.' Rita Mae Brown, writer

NURTURE NEW HABITS

Being busy, busy, busy all the time can lead to the feeling that life is just one demanding task after another. Making time to relax is a crucial part of taking charge of your life. If you're overloaded, a pattern of excessive worrying and blowing small chores out of all proportion quickly develops.

## *Activity*

### Relax: stop doing and try being for a while

Today carve out 20 minutes for yourself away from distractions and do nothing. Sit in the garden, lie on the bed, turn off the phones, the TV and even the radio and enjoy the peace and calm. Take a luxurious bath if you prefer to unwind this way. Forget ironing and calls that need returning. Let all your stresses drift away ...

### TOP TIP

♦ Multi-tasking is a fashionable concept but is it the best strategy? Not always. Focusing on one thing at a time is often a more effective way to complete jobs. Don't try and hold a phone call and do other tasks simultaneously. The other person will sense it!

♦ Write down any worries or reminders for the next day before you go to bed. That way, they won't clutter up your mind.

♦ Be kind to yourself. Don't waste any time beating yourself up if disorder raises its ugly head from time to time. Instead of worrying, do something, no matter how small, to gain control.

♦ Picture each task as a block of Parmesan cheese that you're going to shave into thin slices. Deal with each sliver independently. Taking action will unblock the sensation of being overwhelmed and ticking off completed jobs is a great way to underline your progress.

## *Activity*
# Count your blessings

If you're striving non-stop for the newest car or state-of-the art computer, it's easy to forget that there are more important issues in life, like health, relationships and simple pleasures like watching the sunset.

At bedtime, think of:

- three things you're grateful for today – like having fun with friends, enjoying a swim and watching a good film

- three tasks you accomplished today. These can be cooking delicious spaghetti, filing your tax return or sending a thank-you card to your aunt. Celebrating your achievements every day will build your sense of confidence and help you to move forward.

'Reflect on your present blessings, of which every man has many; not on your past misfortunes, of which all men have some.' Charles Dickens, novelist

There's something addictive and deeply pleasing about letting go of unwanted stuff. Even if the act of decluttering will never be your bliss, it's truly energising to live in a gorgeous home.

## *Activity*

### Adopt simple routines to keep clutter at bay

Now that you've got the upper hand with your clutter, do you suspect that, within a few months, chaos will have engulfed your home again? Banish this fear by staying on top of things on a daily and weekly basis. It's so much harder to deal with a backlog than with a handful of stray or excess items.

**Do**

- Spend half an hour every Saturday morning clearing one small area.

- Once a month, dedicate a full morning or afternoon to a larger project. Always choose a quiet time when you're not going to be interrupted. Schedule this time into your diary.

- Keep a charity bag on the go so you have somewhere for unwanted items. Take it to the shop as soon as it's full.

- Handle things only once – file your new car insurance policy straight away rather than leaving it on the coffee table.

- Know your own energy levels – are you a morning or evening person? Choose your most productive time to get organised.

- Celebrations, Christmas and birthdays will create an influx of new things. This is always a good time to have a decluttering session to keep the balance in your home.

NURTURE NEW HABITS

- Take urgent action if bad habits start to re-emerge like hoarding newspapers or shuffling clutter from room to room, rather than getting rid of it.

- Get help. Can you delegate any of the routine tasks like ironing to a cleaner? Make sure everyone in your household is pulling their weight.

## TOP TIP

If you feel you're constantly short of time, adopt one of these strategies:
- Get up ten minutes earlier.
- Ditch one indifferent TV programme a week.
- Limit your TV and online time every day.
- Have a day each weekend when you don't turn on the TV or computer.
- One day a week, don't read the newspaper – listen to the radio instead while you're doing some tidying up.
- One weekend a month, only buy essentials such as food.
- Text or chat less on your phone.

## Frustration alert!

If clutter is creeping back, you'll start to lose things and feel out of control. This is your warning sign to take action and make sure you're allocating enough time in your schedule for clearouts.

NURTURE NEW HABITS

# Your notes

# CHAPTER 18

# MAINTAIN
# MOTIVATION

Remember that no previous generation faced such consumerist pressures or busy multi-tasking lives. If you've struggled to win the battle with clutter, don't feel you have to go it alone. At difficult times like divorce, bereavement, moving house or the imminent birth of a child, it can be invaluable to have someone by your side.

*Activity*

## Get help to ease your decluttering journey

Choose the right support to help you stay motivated.

### Getting professional help

Visit The Association for Professional Declutterers and Organisers UK at: www.apdo-uk.co.uk for details of declutterers working in your area.

### A clutter buddy

In the past have people treated you as a joke – someone who was born messy or lazy? These attitudes won't encourage you to become more organised. Counter them by finding a clutter buddy – a friend who's also keen to transform their home.

*Do*

- Phone each other once a week and report on progress.
- Laugh at each other's weird and wonderful hoarding ways.
- Share a pitch at a boot fair.
- Ask your buddy to come over and give you a hand on awkward jobs and then you can do the same for them in future.

- Share research on charities that collect and other local resources.

This will work well with the right person but do:

- Beware of 'vultures' who are keen to get hold of your discarded stuff. If they want something for themselves, they're unlikely to give impartial advice!

- Be cautious about making a family member your buddy. If your mum or brother is an incorrigible hoarder, then they'll try to convince you to keep things!

**Clutter help online**

Simply type 'clutter' or 'home organisation' (or 'organization') into the search engines and check out what's available.

www.nomoreclutter.co.uk My website has a wealth of information to smooth your journey from hoarder to order. Register for a free monthly newsletter, and check out the monthly tip and useful links.

## TOP TIP

Whatever support you choose, never ask anyone else's permission about the fate of your own possessions. Whether it was a gift, a family heirloom or it cost mega bucks trust yourself and do what feels right for you.

## Simplify one area of your life

Research shows that people feel increasingly busy and overloaded, which can lead to enormous stress. Every day, we're bombarded by information, new products hit the market hourly and even choosing a flavour of yoghurt can be overwhelming!

But being busy is seen as a status symbol in our society. We're under pressure to work long hours to buy the latest consumer goods and take expensive holidays. In response to this never-ending cycle, many people are choosing to adopt a simpler way of life. There's no need to move to the country, or live without mod cons or the comforts of 21st century living. Small adjustments to your habits can make a big difference to the quality of your everyday life.

### Activity

## Overload quiz

Find out if you need to simplify your life by taking today's quiz. Score 1 for each 'yes':

- Do your feel busy all the time?

- Do you arrange classes and outings for your kids most days?

- Do you find yourself spending a lot of money on convenience food, takeaway coffees and emergency purchases because you're always in a rush?

- Do you wish you had more time to call friends or visit family?

- Do you use retail therapy to alleviate the tensions in your life?

**Your score**

If you score two or more, you must be feeling under a lot of stress. Remedy this by choosing one relaxing habit.

- Turn the TV off this evening and make those calls.

- Instead of shopping in your lunch hour go to a free concert or gallery. Or just sit on a bench and watch the world go by. You'll save money and unwind.

- Drop one unrewarding activity. Don't feel pressure to reschedule that time right away. Leave it open and do something spontaneous instead.

- If you spend hours chauffeuring your kids about, limit the number of activities each week. Like adults, kids are caught up in a culture of hectic schedules. They also need down time just to hang out.

- Before you buy something expensive, calculate how many hours you had to work to buy it. Is it really worth a day's graft to buy another gadget?

- Get up ten minutes earlier and make a coffee rather than rushing to the local coffee shop and getting impatient in the queue.

'Normal is getting dressed in clothes that you buy for work and driving through traffic in a car that you're still paying for – in order to get to the job that you need to pay for the clothes and the car and the house you leave vacant all day so you can afford to live in it.' Ellen Goodman, Pullitzer Prize-winning writer

MAINTAIN MOTIVATION

Is all the jumble and junk a fading memory? If it is, that's fantastic! Enjoy revelling in the reality of your newly organised home.

## *Activity*

## Clarify how far you've come

Write down the following:

### Your successes

- All the improvements you've made throughout your home.

- Rooms or sections of rooms you feel particularly proud of.

- Any compliments you've received on your decluttered home.

- Routines you've adopted like opening the post daily or giving one-read novels to the charity shop. Developing and maintaining new habits is a huge achievement.

- Look back at the negative words such as 'clutterbug' or 'overloaded' that you wrote down on Day 1. Find new words that are more appropriate for you today like 'smart shopper', 'recycler' and 'free from clutter'.

### Your plans for the future

Set realistic goals that will sustain your clutter-free life. So make a note of:

- any untouched areas like the cellar or videos

- any hoarding habits (keeping odd socks or yoghurt pots) that you haven't got to grips with yet

MAINTAIN MOTIVATION

- any specific tasks that you find daunting – if yours is sentimental belongings, then gently push yourself but accept it's tough for you right now

- any places that you feel would benefit from a second clearout. Decluttering happens in phases – now that you're more comfortable with the process, streamline a little more.

## Yes but ...

Perhaps you feel that party poppers are premature and that persistent pockets of clutter, like your paperwork are still a worry. In the real world, unless you have a team of staff on 24-hour alert, a perfect home is unlikely to last more than a minute.

From time to time, things will drift towards chaos, for example, if you go down with flu, there's a family crisis or an urgent project. But that won't in any way undermine all the positive progress you've made. The difference now is you know that you can restore order quickly.

## Encourage yourself

Remember, your home has been transformed by small daily steps. If you persevere with this little-and-often approach, you'll continue to improve and enjoy your living space.

Don't ever underestimate your efforts. Be pleased with every move you take towards the life you want. A tidy wardrobe may not change the world but it will free you to concentrate on what really matters to you – whether it's getting fit, running an after-school club or learning to meditate.

'Maybe the most any of us can expect of ourselves isn't perfection but progress.' Michelle Burford, journalist

MAINTAIN MOTIVATION

It's not easy to alter lifelong habits and you've had the courage, determination and commitment to do just that. Congratulations!

## Activity

### Acknowledge all your achievements

One last quick task to complete. This quiz will underline just how many positive changes you've made!

**Hoarder to Order quiz**

Count 1 point for each statement you agree with.

- I feel less stressed and more in control.

- I take pleasure in spending time in clutter-free areas in my home.

- I no longer see myself as an incurable hoarder.

- I can find most things quickly and without drama.

- I accept that possessions flow through my life.

- I find letting go of things easier than I did 100 days ago.

- People have remarked on the positive changes.

- Perfect homes are fictional. My aim is to truly enjoy my home.

- Little and often is the way forward for decluttering.

- I'm never going to get as disorganised again.

- I have the skills and understanding to maintain order in my life.

- I'm wasting less money on things I don't need.

- I'm using and enjoying my things more and I'm no longer saving them for a rainy day.

- I'm not possessed by my possessions any more.

- I'm proud of my determination, my hard work and all my achievements over the last 100 days.

**Your score**

Over 10: You're feeling good and you deserve to!

Under 10: You're being pretty down on yourself. Relax and remember how much you've accomplished.

## Celebrate

Get the champagne on ice and toast your successes. Raise your glass to your new organised life. Cheers …

**⊙← TOP TIP**

Repeat this clutter-free mantra: 'Every day I'm making progress towards a clutter-free and orderly life.'

# Your notes

# FURTHER INFORMATION

For more information on Sue Kay and *No More Clutter*, visit www.nomoreclutter.co.uk and register for a free newsletter.

## Decluttering help

**www.apdo–uk.co.uk**
The Association of Professional Declutterers and Organisers UK for help in your area.

**www.clutterersanonymous.net**
This follows the 12-step approach. Their spiritual approach to overcoming clutter sees hoarding as a manifestation of deeper problems.

**www.flylady.net**
This site sends out tips to help you fly in your battle against clutter.

**www.messies.com**
This is an active website with online support groups and useful tips.

## Extreme hoarding

For severe problems with hoarding, first speak to your GP. There may be underlying medical conditions such as obsessive compulsive disorder (OCD), attention deficit disorder (ADD) or depression.

**www.addiss.co.uk**
The National Attention Deficit Disorder Information and Support Service

**www.ocdaction.org.uk**
This national organisation offers advice and support for people experiencing obsessive compulsive disorder.

## Support organisations

**www.bacp.co.uk**
The British Association of Counselling and Psychotherapy has a list of qualified therapists and counsellors.

**www.adviceguide.org.uk**
The Citizens' Advice Bureau offers support on managing debt problems.

**www.crusebereavementcare.org.uk**
Contact CRUSE for help following bereavement.
National helpline 0870 167 1677.

**www.nationaldebtline.co.uk**
This organisation offers help if your compulsive shopping has led to financial problems. Freephone 0808 808 4000.

**www.relate.org.uk**
Relate offers counselling and workshops if clutter is causing a problem in your relationship.

## Donating

**www.charitychoice.co.uk**
This site has a directory of charities if you want to give directly to a community group.

**www.charityshops.org.uk**
Visit this site and click on 'Find a Charity Shop'.

**www.freecycle.org**
This organisation will give advice on donating your goods for free.

## Swapping sites

Swap your unwanted clutter for something useful.
**www.swapthelot.co.uk**
**www.swapxchange.org**

## Selling

**www.amazon.co.uk**
Try Amazon for selling books and CDs.

**www.carbootcalendar.com**
This website lists car boot sales around the UK.

**www.ebay.co.uk**
Try the online auction site.

**www.yell.co.uk**
This site is a great source for locating second-hand shops.

## Antiques

For advice on selling antiques and for reputable dealers, try the following websites:

**www.bada.org**
The British Antique Dealers Association

**www.bbc.co.uk/antiques**
For general information on antiques and the best way to sell them.

**www.lapada.co.uk**
The Association of Art and Antique Dealers

## Recycling

There are many organisations that can recycle and re-use your things:

**www.childrensscrapstore.co.uk**
Check out this site to find all sorts of recycling for children's play things.

**www.computersforcharity.org.uk**
This organisation will recondition your old PC and give it to a charity.

**www.frn.org.uk**
The Furniture Reuse Network can help pass on your furniture and appliances to people on low incomes.

**www.recycle-more.co.uk**
Visit this site for general recycling information.

**www.vao.org.uk**
You can send your old spectacles to Vision Aid Overseas, but do check with your local optician first because many collect them in store.

Numerous organisations, including the Body Shop, Crisis, Orange and Oxfam recycle mobile phones to raise money for charity.

## Simple living

**www.presentaid.org** and **www.oxfamunwrapped.com**
Visit these websites for great ethical gifts like goats and cans of worms for distribution and use in a developing country.

**www.buynothingday.co.uk**
Once a year, give your wallet a rest.

**www.mpsonline.org.uk**
Mail preference service – to stop junk mail wasting your time.

**www.simpleliving.net**
Tips on how to declutter your life.

## Storage solutions

You're spoilt for choice when it comes to storage. Department stores such as John Lewis or DIY superstores have a wide range of products.

**www.theholdingcompany.co.uk**
The Holding Company sells stylish storage you'll enjoy using.

**www.lakelandlimited.co.uk**
For vacuum packs, anti–moth products, over-the-door hooks and much more.

**www.muji.co.uk**
Muji sells transparent products so you can see what you've stored.

**www.bpca.org.uk**
Get in touch with the British Pest Control Association if you have a serious moth infestation.

# RECOMMENDED READING

Here are some excellent books on clutter and related topics:

Aslett, D. (1995) *Clutter Free! Finally and Forever*, Don Betterway Books
Emmett, R. (2000) *The Procrastinator's Handbook*, Walker Publishing
Felton, S. (2000) *The New Messies Manual*, Revel
Glovinsky, C. (2002) *Making Peace with the Things in Your Life*, St Martin's Press
Hall, A. (2002) *Your Money or Your Life*, Coronet
Kay, S. (2005) *No More Clutter*, Hodder Mobius
Kingston, K. (1998) *Clear Your Clutter with Feng Shui*, Piatkus
Luhrs, J. (1997) *The Simple Living Guide*, Broadway Books
Mamen, M. (2006) *The Pampered Child Syndrome*, Jessica Kingsley
Schor, J. (1998) *The Overspent American*, Harper Collins

# Why not
## try another title in the series?

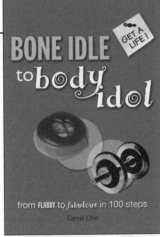

**BONE IDLE to BODY IDOL**
0-340-90799-1

**MOODY to MELLOW**
0-340-90801-7

**DRAB to FAB**
0-340-90804-1

**SINGLE to SETTLED**
0-340-90800-9